R.F. DELDERFIELD
BUTTERFLY MOMENTS
(1912 – 1972)

THE BIOGRAPHY OF A QUINTESSENTIAL ENGLISH WRITER

CENTENARY EDITION
with extensive new material

MARION LINDSEY-NOBLE

Cashmere Publishing

CASHMERE PUBLISHING
High Meadow House, Brompton Regis, Somerset, TA22 9NW
marion.lindsey-noble@btinternet.com

ISBN 978 0 95579322 6

Printed and bound in Great Britain by Booksprint

DEDICATION

This biography is dedicated to the memory of R.F. Delderfield, the most prolific and entertaining author of his time, a most devoted ambassador for England, in particular for the West Country, and a delightful Englishman.

PART 1

THE BIOGRAPHY OF A QUINTESSENTIAL ENGLISH WRITER

CONTENTS

ACKNOWLEDGEMENTS

There are a great many peoople to thank for their loyal support during the years of research.

I owe a debt in particular to R.F. Delderfield's friends in Exmouth and Sidmouth; the late Mr. Bill Sleeman, the late Queenie Greenaway, Kay Gibbons and Roy Moxy spring to mind immediately. We had a wonderful time reminiscing, and they were still going strong after midnight when I was flagging.

The late Peter Ely of 'Delderfield's' in Sidmouth was helpful and a great support and Patricia Avery invited me to tell me about her 'hunt' encounters with the author.

The late Mr. Geoffrey Woodhead and his wife Carol, of Honiton and their son-in-law Phillip Massell gave freely of their time to share memories.

The late Robert Russell, R.F. Delderfield's closest friend and admirer in the RAF wrote down all his memories of 'Delder' and I can't thank him and his wife Audrey enough!

A surprising number of people replied to my advertisements in RAF magazines and local newspapers; it was so kind of you all and added many pieces to the puzzle. Thank you.

Newspaper archivists and West Country libraries were amazingly helpful and the "The Grange's" and West Buckland's archivists were so generous in letting me have materials dug out from old files in vaults. Thank you.

Mr. Sean Noel of Boston University rediscovered the use of envelopes (rather than e-mails) sending me an entire inventory of their special R.F. Delderfield collection. I am glad to add this biography to it.

Robin Denniston and Eric and Pauline McKenzie, ex Hodder & Stoughton greats, were wonderful to listen to. Sorry being late for lunch, Robin.

Thank you, Roy Ware for letting me have your collection and for your hospitality.

Bob Delderfield of Essex replied with enthusiasm which was reinforcing my determination.

Mr. John S. Sermon deserves a special mention for sharing memories of his meeting with R.F. Delderfield and expressing enthusiastic support.

Veronica and Richard Persse, daughter and son-in-law of R.F. Delderfield were encouraging from the start and tremendously helpful once we had established contact. I hope I have done justice to your family's history, and a warm 'thank you'.

Lastly, an acknowledgement to my husband Royce who very patiently spent many evenings on his own while I was busy in my study sorting and writing. He is such a generous, helpful and kind man, driving me to meetings, supplying me with a constant flow of cups of tea and listening endlessly to my findings and ideas. It has neither gone unnoticed nor been taken for granted. A big thank you and a hug!

There are many more names I could include if space permitted. Please feel included in my warmest of thanks and appreciation.

ONE

All Over The Town and *Ben Gunn*
(1945-1954)

'Daddy, Daddy!'
The din of the arriving train cannot mask the excited, high pitched voice of eighteen months old Veronica, as she toddles, holding her mother's hand, along the platform of Exmouth station. They have been waiting since May for the day, when Ron Delderfield would be demobbed to return home to his loved ones in the West Country. Today is the fourth of November, a happy day, in spite of the steady drizzle outside and a grey, cloud-laden sky.

Many other families share this moment, and little Veronica is not sure into whose arms she should throw herself. She is too young to remember her daddy from the infrequent and short visits during the first year with her adoptive family.

Her mother bends down and whispers in her ear: 'There he is,' and points through a gap in the crowd at a tall, slim man with vivid blue eyes behind black-rimmed glasses whose face is bathed in smiles. He puts down his bag and opens his arms. Veronica needs no more confirmation.

'Daddy,' the word drowns in her gurgling laughter as she runs confidently towards him and disappears in his rough coat, her little nose buried in the smell of mothballs, stale cigarette smoke and comforting warmth.

May Delderfield watches the pair with deep love and contentment. Her blue eyes sparkle as they haven't sparkled in a long time. Ron kisses his wife heartily on the mouth, squashing Veronica in their embrace. Forgotten are the war years which separated them; put to rest are the three still-births that May suffered and which have left deep scars in both their hearts.

Ron's return to 'civvy street' marks the start of a new life.

They decide to treat themselves and hire a taxi. During the ride to their house called Oak Park in Bradham Lane, Veronica doesn't stop chattering and the parents are happy to oblige, giving her their full attention.

'Now that we are three, we really need to look for a bigger house,' May suggests as she hangs up her hat, scarf and coat in the narrow landing of Oak Park house and peels her little girl out of layers of winter clothing.

Ron chuckles. He knows how May manages to fill a house with her finds from antique shops and fairs; how her water colours and oil paintings take over a suite of rooms.

However, he couldn't wish for a more supportive wife and it gives him pleasure to indulge her wish. If everything goes according to plan his theatre play *Worm's Eye View* will open at the Embassy Theatre in London in December.

He smiles at his little family. 'You go ahead and find us a nice place,' he agrees cheerfully.

Soon after his return, Ron needs to meet up urgently with Ronnie Shiner, the star of *Worm's Eye View*. He takes the train back up to London and combines the trip with a visit to his agent Juliet O'Hea of Curtis Brown, who is interested in the stories he has written about Margaret of Anjou, the wife of Henry VI.

Ron is not keen to leave the West Country and finds the trips to confer with directors, producers and actors not only intrusive in his writing routine and private life, but also financially ruinous considering that nothing has really earned him a fortune so far.

Ronnie Shiner, who never stopped believing that *Worm's Eye View* would be a success, is eventually proved right. The play opens on the fourth of December as planned for two weeks. It is then transferred to the Whitehall Theatre just before Christmas, where it shares a double bill with *Fit For Heroes*.

Further reports from London's West End sound gloomy and Ron isn't sure what he can do about it.

Suddenly, the messages become more positive. Audience figures build up through recommendations by word of mouth and by mid-spring 1946, the play nets over £2,000 a week.

Ron is over the moon and May smiles at him with pride. She has great hopes that they might be able to afford to move.

The euphoria doesn't last long. Another problem arises: the cast loses the lease. Their agent comes up with the idea to send the play on tour for nine weeks hoping, he can sort out another venue.

However, the tour is such a success that the Whitehall Theatre offers to put the play back on its stage. There it will stay for five years and seven months.

The Delderfields have indeed moved house in March 1946 to St.

Cyr in Douglas Avenue. It has three bedrooms and is located on the outskirts of Exmouth. They also buy a second hand Ford with the first proceeds from the play. When May hears about a little boy called Paul who needs a family, they volunteer and adopt him as a brother to Veronica.

Once it becomes clear that *Worm's Eye View* is going to be a great success, the Delderfields start giving parties for their local and London friends and buy a second hand Daimler from the local dealer, Mr. Boobyer. They are generous hosts although they do not always find a lot in common with the London theatre folk. May is sometimes found napping on the settee, if the party goes on until late in the night.

Between writing more plays and adaptations for radio and TV, Ron keeps very much in contact with his army friends. He doesn't want to lose them. Their shared memories of the war years are still fresh, and many RAF colleagues like w/o Smale, L.W. and A.G. Tennant Moon visit him in Devon. Mr. Tennant Moon, artist and principal of Cumbria College of Art and Design in Carlisle, stays longer than most because he has been given a commission to paint a family portrait.

Ron is also trying his hand at writing a novel about life and work at a provincial newspaper. It is a veiled attempt at fleeing the theatre world. *All Over The Town* evolves from a play Ron had written as far back as 1932, when he called it *Fleet Street in Lilliput*. He had used his experience as a reporter on his father's local newspaper, The *Exmouth Chronicle* and wrote about journalism in a small seaside town and Nat Hurst's fight to turn the Sandcombe and District Post from a sleepy and sycophantic rag into a live newspaper.

The novel is eventually published in 1947, but does not attract much interest. However the stage version experiences a revival.

The play had been briefly performed in late July 1939 under the title *Printer's Devil* at the Q Theatre, but even then Ron was taken aback by the terrible tensions behind stage and he was often furious because the actors constantly asked him to re-write scenes. The play's success was muted and it was soon forgotten.

During the war, *Printer's Devil* had amused various RAF camps, when Ron had cajoled everyone to perform it on improvised stages, but that was more for fun, to keep up moral and to forget that there was a war on.

On 16th June 1947, the play begins a second run under Ron's old friends, Basil Thomas and Derek Salberg in Wolverhampton. It is ecstatically received by the Wulfrunian audience and extracts rave reviews:

'Mr. Delderfield has a considerable knowledge of local politics and a quick eye for local politicians. His play is a good honest piece of work. Walter Hudd plays Nat with the honesty the part demands. It could be hardly better done. Curigwen Lewis plays his fiancée with tact and charm, and there is good work by Arthur Young, Eliot Makeham, William Hellbroun and half a dozen others.'

From Wolverhampton, *Printer's Devil* transfers to the Playhouse Theatre in London on October 21st under the direction of Terence De Marney, with a star-studded cast including Peter Neil, Rosalyn Boulter, Richard Carr, Gordon Philditt, Peter Scott, Alec Finter, Arthur Seaton and Sydney Monckton.

The reaction of the audience is considerably more positive than some of the reviews, like the one in the *Theatre World*, which can only admit to 'some freshness in seeing a small community reflected in terms of its local paper valiantly fighting for its soul.'

Ron likes to write something with a social message, something that makes people think. In August 1947, he admits in an interview to Peter Drake of the *Western Morning News*:

'I feel strongly that it is possible to establish an important social theme within the framework of laughter.'

However, his main aim is to make people laugh, wanting to entertain them without causing offence.

'I am a humorist rather than a satirist,' Ron says, 'the difference being that the humorist likes the people he playfully debunks.'

Ron works less now for his father's newspaper, the *Exmouth Chronicle*. It has dominated his life for most of his adulthood. It has given him the apprenticeship as a writer. Ron had always preferred to be the observer rather than the subject of interest and finds it strange that *Worm's Eye View* has brought him enough fame to be asked to open bazaars, to judge fancy-dress parades, to address Rotary Clubs and Women's Institutes, to be a subject for newspaper articles and to be interviewed.

When Mr. Delderfield senior retires in 1947, the *Exmouth Chronicle* is sold to Sir Geoffrey Harmsworth from the Air Ministry. All that is left is the printing press run by Ron's brother Eric. In one sense, Ron feels relieved that he will be able to concentrate solely on his play-writing and historical novels. However, he feels immediate regret at missing the constant contact with the West Country people who live around him, who made wonderful subjects for his newspaper articles and whose causes he had sternly defended.

'I won't have to give up the latter,' Ron thinks to himself. 'There are plenty of requests from local newspapers to write articles about topics that are close to my heart.'

In 1950, the Delderfields move again, to a house called – aptly named for Ron, the resident Napoleon enthusiast – St Cyr in Douglas Avenue in Exmouth. However the family live there only a year before they go house-hunting eastwards along the coast at Pebblecombe Regis. The new house is called 'Spion Kop'. It only needs a few touches and is situated high up on the cliffs of Budleigh Salterton. However, a year later, they decide that they need more space to keep animals. They buy the leasehold of Knowle House, a small holding which is in a sorry state. The builders are there for months and during that bitterly cold winter, Ron finds himself writing *Seven Men of Gascony*, the story of Napoleon's Grand Army, wrapped in two dressing gowns and a rug around his feet.

He shares the house not only with his wife and children, but also with Phyllis the factotum and the family pet terrier, Punch, who sleeps on the bedroom rug and snores like an elderly harmonium.

Just after the move, Ron's mother dies quietly after a long illness. Ron has never been particularly close to her until in later years when he encouraged his children to visit granny frequently. The two brothers, Ron and Eric are delighted when their father marries soon afterwards an old widowed friend of the family, a quiet lady who understands and appreciates Delderfield Senior's irrepressible temperament. It suits the brothers fine that their father continues to be so independent-minded in spite of the suspicion that the new Mrs. Delderfield is particularly fond of her husband's money. Ron and May give a lunch party for the newly weds, but see a lot less of Grandpa after he remarried.

Knowle House is a wonderful property and the space entices the family to try their hands at farming, which they hope will also supplement the food rations allocated to them. It is actually May, who Ron thinks comes from farming stock, who brings up this idea. It doesn't happen at once, they slide slowly into it.

At first, they go out to buy hens, but they return with hens and one cow. They call her Christine and explain their surprise purchase with the feeble excuse that 'Christine had such nice red hooves and a white patch on her back, which looks like a map of Madagascar.'

Soon afterwards, they buy three Guernsey cows to provide company for Christine. They think this is financially shrewd and apply for a milk licence, but this turns out to be trickier than they had expected. In spite of this setback, May becomes an expert at making Devonshire cream and butter and ultimately acquires a T.T. licence from the Ministry of Agriculture.

The free-range hens are soon put into battery, because the family spends hours every day trying to find the eggs. However, even the batteries prove troublesome, because the eggs don't roll down the trays and the hens look unhappy, too.

Next the Delderfields buy ducks. The problem with them is immediately apparent: they raid the hen pellets.

'We must cut down on the ducks,' May suggests.

When they do, they are left with one drake and fifteen wives and none of them produces a duckling.

The children, Veronica and Paul, are delighted when a pig is bought. 'Little Audrey', the pig that will not grow, however much it is fed, proves another expensive if interesting experiment. Two more pig-additions, called 'Eggs' and 'Bacon' turn out equally unprofitable because nobody ever has the heart to send them to slaughter.

A trial run with grey geese is unsuccessful because everyone is frightened of them.

They intimidate the entire family and little Veronica calls them 'The Awfuls'. Her pony 'Velvet' is kept in a field at the far side of the geese. Only young Paul dares to attack them to protect his sister. He rushes at them with a dustbin lid and a long broom and manages to put them to flight on most occasions. A major drawback to his strategy is that Veronica can outrun the geese, but that the little knight with the dustbin lid is slower than the birds. It is a glorious shambles. The geese pen acquires the name of 'The Valley of the Honking Death.'

The only animals that bring unbridled pleasure, particularly to Veronica, are their horses 'Velvet' and 'Coalmine'. The little girl has a natural talent for riding and soon becomes devoted and completely smitten.

Luckily, they have found and employed a loyal and hard-working local man, Ron Hole, to help them. He had applied for the job of general handyman and gardener in 1951, because he planned to get married and had hopes of installing his young wife in the cottage in the grounds of Knowle House.

He soon finds himself solely in charge of the entire estate including the farm-zoo, seeing to it that the house, family and assorted creatures are ticking over nicely. He often shakes his head about the Delderfield's amateur enthusiasm, but can't help being terribly fond of them.

His days start at seven o'clock, when he wakes up his employer by whistling *The Third Man* and brings him a cup of tea. The family have breakfast at eight after which Ron Hole gets on with estate business and Ron Delderfield retires into his study to deal with correspondence until ten and then to write until one o'clock. The family might then go out together for long walks on the beach or in the countryside or, occasionally, father will change into his pink riding attire and either join the East Devon Fox Hunt or ask his handyman to accompany him riding in the surrounding area.

Little does the author know that the hunting fraternity snigger a little behind his back. He isn't really entitled to wearing the pink outfit, but they feel that he is such a lovely man, that nobody has the heart to tell him.[1] They certainly prefer him to his pompous brother Eric, who comes along sometimes, 'a man irritating beyond measure', who seems to be in constant competition with his brother without having his talent nor his sociability.

They are unaware that Eric is successful in his own way. He is chairman of the Exmouth Town Council and writes books like *The Kings and Queens of England*, animal stories and the Exmoor Ordnance Survey maps. Of course, this brings not the same kind of popularity Ron has achieved with his kind and jovial nature and West End success, but the brothers get on well without living in each others' pocket.

The children riding behind the hunting adults see the author as a source of amusement, a well-padded gentleman at the very end of the adult group on horseback, just ahead of them. They watch him, his legs dangling – because they are far too long for the size of his horse – swaying from side to side, and they wait in suspense whether he will fall off again.

---

1. His daughter Veronica assures me that her father only changed from his black jacket after the Hunt gave him his hunt buttons after several years of hunting with the East Devon. He was extremely proud of this honour for it entitled him to wear 'Pink'. Veronica was one of the children hunting and was not aware of any sniggering. Her daddy was rarely at the back of the field, unless he wanted to check on his daughter. The only time he fell off, she says, was when his girth broke; he was quite badly hurt as his horse stood on him which left him with a perfect shoe print on his thigh.

Ron in turn likes the mixture of professional men, farmers and farmers' sons, who look easy-going and out to enjoy themselves, although he does not get to know many people well.[2]

'I don't understand their strange conversations and some of the ladies look terrifying,' he admits.

When not out riding with the Hunt, Ron asks Ron Hole to accompany him. His 'Man Friday', as he calls him, is not always keen because his mind is really more on things to do with the estate. He knows that he will have to listen to the most recent developments in his employer's stories, who will talk incessantly, bouncing off ideas. Even then, engrossed in spinning his yarn, the author sometimes falls off his horse and returns plastered in mud.

May, who is always cheerful and appreciative of Ron Hole's work, is wise not to come to these outings. She does not enjoy riding and prefers, when she is not busy with the children, to paint still-lifes and to look after a little antiques shop in the old Toll House on Holden Hill on the Plymouth Road.

Two or three times a week, the couple go to the cinema to indulge in their old passion, whilst the children are looked after by Sheila Franks, a kind neighbour who is very fond of the children. Veronica is known to be a little devil and definitely a daddy's girl and already quite an accomplished horse-lady, whilst young Paul is not an easy child and rather beyond his parents' experience, in spite of all the love lavished on both children.

In the fairly chaotic household, Paul maybe misses out on the specific care and attention he needs, unable to compete with his sparkling older sister. The parents have always prided themselves that they are no disciplinarians and are fiercely set against any, particularly corporal, punishment. Admittedly, the children live by clearly defined rules with punishments such as no bedtime story or no pocket money, but Paul might have benefited from a little more firm guidance in his childhood and from being given goals and expectations to fulfil.[3]

Luckily, Ron loves children.

---

2. According to Veronica, the family had many friends among the hunting fraternity. The children were involved in the lunch time parties while Ron and May attended many evening gatherings.

3. According to his sister, Paul was, as a small boy, very easy, happy and outgoing. It was not until his teens that he started to become difficult. Veronica is convinced that Paul suffered for most of his adulthood from the fact that his natural mother had given him away. He simply could not forgive her and never understood how difficult it was for an unmarried mother in the 1940s.

'The more children who are about the better I like it,' he assures May. 'They give me great stimulus to an honest approach to humanity; they are themselves the greatest debunkers in the world.'

Dad's tapping on the typewriter resounding through the house in the mornings and often for another couple of hours before supper, becomes the children's most cherished childhood sound.

Reminiscent of the time when he was a little boy, who used to keep strict accounts when he lent money to his two older brothers, the family man Ron Delderfield still tries to keep track of the family spending. He doesn't always succeed because it is more important to him not to appear mean..

'Not you again,' he quips, when his Man Friday arrives on payday to collect his wages. They all know that they cannot do without him. Apart from running the estate, he is the one to knock up a sledge, on which Paul, Veronica and their father huddle and zoom down slopes under squeals of laughter and mock fright; they leave it now to him to set up the fireworks on November 5th, after one year, father and son nearly burnt down the estate with an almighty explosion.

By 1954, the assorted collection of creatures in the grounds of Knowle House becomes too much to handle. The Delderfields are not particularly aware of this and only after Ron Hole, their 'Man Friday' threatens to leave and the accountant predicts ruin, they decide to part with the majority of the menagerie. Ron Hole tells his wife with horror that the Delderfields have lost £2,000 on that farm, which is an awful lot of money in the 1950s. His own weekly pay is only £20.[4]

It is time to be sensible and cut costs. They had spent a lot of money on improving Knowle House and when the time comes to renegotiate the leasehold, Clinton Devon estates want much more money. Rationing is over, so there is no need for the assorted farm animals. The Delderfield's move to Shortwood House in Budleigh Salterton's Beare Lane.

'It feels like the disembarkation of Noah's Ark on Mount Ararat,' Ron moans theatrically, comparing his family with 'war-ravaged peasants watching the receding tide of an army occupation'.

May is also a little subdued. She likes the idea of being a hobby farmer, but they have never managed to be business-like and have perhaps gone over the top this time.

---

4. Veronica agrees that her father was never good with money. She remembers how, on one occasion, they were shopping for Mummy's birthday present. He chose an expensive watch which he thought would suit her perfectly. He muttered that he couldn't really afford it, but bought it anyway.

'Let's take one cow and the horses,' she suggests. 'That way, we can still use the membership card of the Farmers' Union and can look professional at agricultural shows.

They were also joined by May's father and his second wife Jessie, who occupied a separate flat.

From time to time, May and Ron's doctor suggests they go on holiday. Ron's relentless writing routine should be off-set by regular breaks and more physical exercise. However, after some disastrous childhood holidays, Ron is not one for leaving his home in search of exotic adventures. He can hardly tear himself away from the West Country:

'There is more warmth, sincerity and honest friendship than anywhere else in the world.' Most of all, he resents when his daily writing routine is interrupted.

In the early 1950s, the doctor and May succeed in luring him away to Switzerland. It rains continuously, they meet mainly English people, May hates flying and riding up the mountain in a funicular railway and the food is too rich and too much.

They try Paris, once with May's niece Wendy, then fifteen. This is more fun. Ron thinks that he and May are a good team when it comes to speaking French.

'I know most of the words but I can't pronounce them, while she has an exquisite accent, but can never remember the words. Consequently, every time we want to ask a question, we have to do a sort of music-hall act and usually the person we have accosted has walked away before we have worked out the sentence.'

The children are taken to Paris on another occasion and relish staying in their parent's favourite hotel and being shown their favourite sights.

The Parisian taxi drivers frighten the couple to death and so do the bus drivers along coastal highways during an Italian trip.

Another trip to Italy is ruined when their brand-new Daimler car develops an oil leak. while the chauffeur drives them along the Riviera. As they were only allowed to take £50 out of the country, most of their holiday money is spent on oil.

Ron is sent alone on a walking holiday to Ireland to counteract his unhealthy, sedentary life-style. He hates it and the loneliness and exertion do not improve his health as they are meant to do. The knapsack cuts into his kidneys and once he has sung all the songs and tunes he can remember along the first miles, he gives up. In spite of feelings of guilt towards those having stayed behind, hoping he would get himself fit, he accepts a lift and heads for home. It is his last attempt at a holiday abroad.

From then on, he sticks to a daily regime of riding, walking and swimming. Even when he is in London, he uses the hotel swimming pool.

In 1953, Ron's play *Worm's Eye View* finally closes its doors and the author is grateful that he is kept busy with more theatre productions and their off-spins:

Spark in Judea, a religious play, is printed and will be televised on Easter Sunday; *The Orchard Walls* is staged at St. Martin's with Gillian Lind, Helen Horsey, Ron Charlesworth and Cyril Raymond;

Follow The Plough opens for one week at the Q Theatre and is featured a few weeks later on television. In 1954, it goes on tour under the new title *Where There Is A Will*.

Peace Comes To Peckham is the Home Service's Saturday play; and the West of England Theatre Company presents his new play *Golden Rain* at the Savoy Theatre in Exmouth. It is adapted and shown on television on the 31st July 1953.

Ron likes *Golden Rain* and thinks it is his best to date.

He writes twelve more plays in the next two years, of which the better known are *The Guinea Pigs*, *The Rounderlay Tradition* (an all women comedy) and *The Queen Came By* which stars the young actresses Jean St. Clair and Thora Hird.

'Too sentimental,' he admits in a letter to his WAAF friend Dora Haken, 'but look at the author.'

'I may also do the TV Christmas play', he writes to her, 'but at the moment I am finishing another three-act and I am doing Shiner's next film. *Where There Is A Will* is rehearsed at the Three Arts Club near Marble Arch and will open at Nottingham on Monday and at Exeter on March 15th. After four weeks in the provinces, it is due in the West End, but no theatre has been found for it so far.'

Two more of his theatre scripts are used for film eventually: *Where There Is A Will* and *The Orchard Walls*, which is released as *Now And Forever*, adapted by Michael Pertwee in co-operation with the author.

Ron also adapts Derrick Boothroyd's novel *Value For Money* with William Fairchild as his co-author.

The Bride Wore An Opal Ring, a play originally inspired by the wedding questionnaire Ron had used while still a local reporter, is adapted for television and broadcast, and in February 1955, Thora Hird plays Emmie Slee in *The Queen Came By* on radio.

The enormous success of *Worm's Eye View* provided the family with a comfortable lifestyle; however, it did pall with time. Now that the play's run has ended, Ron is writing furiously to make up for the shortfall in income and to keep his family finances afloat.

However, none of his subsequent plays experiences the same good fortune and rewards are negligible. It is the 'kitchen sink' plays like *Look Back In Anger*, which are popular now. Ron feels under much pressure and on a treadmill, from which he dare not jump off. Professional satisfaction is waning. His ambivalent impression of the theatre world has not changed, but this is where success lies, although the audiences seem to like his plays better than the critics.

'My heart is not on the stage,' he says to May who has come into his study to supply him with another cup of black coffee. 'The trouble with a lot of modern work is that too often, the strident style obscures an interesting message. People want plays about sex and violence which are only part of life. To me the real hero is the ordinary chap, the middle-aged bank clerk saving up to pay his way, educate his family and keep his head above water.'

'I have never learnt to feel at ease with theatre folk,' he sighs.

'I don't see them as real people either', she agrees, having got to know many of them when they came to their parties at Knowle and Shortwood House.

'They seem to live from hand to mouth; they are foreign to all the people we have ever known…' she muses.

'Quite, I don't think the locals know what to make of them either,' he emphasizes. 'Their gaiety is as brittle as their promises, peppered with bouts of melancholy. They bestow their comradeship lightly, only to discard it when it suits them.'

'That's a bit harsh,' May nibbles at her lower lip.

'Well, that's how I feel,' her husband insists. He turns to take a book from the shelf behind him.

'Shouldn't we be grateful?' she smiles at him. 'We haven't done badly out of them.'

Ron grumbles something unintelligible into his chest, leafing already through the book he has chosen.

'Better leave him to it,' she thinks, hops down from the desk corner she had perched herself on, and throws one more glance at her husband.

He is already engrossed in his next project. While she walks slowly down the stairs, letting her hand glide over the smooth wood of the banister she remembers him grumbling that 'writing plays was not nearly as interesting or so vital as journalism, because it is contrived and made to fit a pattern, imposed by custom and fashion.'

She comes to the conclusion, that Ron is professionally at a cross-roads; he is restless, dissatisfied, and ready to jump ship, and she wonders whether he will return to journalism or decide on something else altogether.

She personally wouldn't mind if he chose the newspaper world again. He was a reporter at his father's *Exmouth Chronicle* when they first met. It was during a youth hostelling holiday in Wales, when her group of Northerners was thrown together with young people from Devon. She remembers the gawky, talkative young man with heavy black rimmed glasses, smuggling himself next to her in a concert ticket queue.

Having arrived at the bottom of the stairs, she smiles to herself: 'Yes, I would like him to be a journalist again,' she thinks before being swallowed up by the demands of the children clamouring for her attention.

TWO

Exmouth, the *Chronicle* and May
(1929 – 1939)

Ron left the public West Buckland Boarding School, situated in the wilds of Exmoor, at the age of sixteen and attended a one year course with more or less success at a Commercial College in Exeter. His life began now in earnest. He was roped in to help with his father's newspaper, the *Exmouth Chronicle* as a cub reporter, while his brother Eric, who had been sent to learn the trade in apprenticeships, was in charge of the printing press.

The *Exmouth Chronicle* was a small town newspaper, whose front page was covered in advertisements and an old-fashioned picture of the Exmouth sea-front in the 1870s.
   Advertisements were the bread and butter of the paper and the demand was usually greater than the space available.
   Ron enjoyed his new role as a cub reporter enormously. He was often an honorary guest at weddings, funerals and baptisms, in the hope that he would give the occasion a colourful and generous write-up. It could be tricky, because it was vital that he got the names right and printed the list of guests or mourners correctly in their order of rank. In his first two years, he found this particularly difficult, as he was still battling to read back his own shorthand.
   It was a steep learning curve, acquiring the diplomatic skills to treat every customer with earnestness and importance, even though Ron might have felt tempted to laugh. Many of his customers' 'gems', uttered quite seriously by locals on such occasions, would re-appear in plays and stories, he wrote in his spare time..
   One family had insisted that the following poem be incorporated into the obituary:
   An angel trumpet sounded,
   An angel voice said 'come',
   The pearly gates they opened wide,
       and in walked Mum!
Being present at funerals brought him face to face with the question of mortality, but he never cared to dwell upon it for too long.

Covering weddings brought some additional complications, because the dresses, guests and grandeur of reception had to be reported in great detail. In summer, when there were a great number of weddings, each family expected an individual description of the festivities that would stand-out from the rest. Ron had to eat and drink himself through large quantities of food and wines and then had to write something original about each of them.

Another source of information to fill columns, were the Petty Sessions. These had made the young reporter rather nervous at first, because it had been pointed out to him that one misrepresentation of facts might spell disaster for the *Chronicle*, but he often found that they provided him with some of the best and snappiest headlines.

There were also country 'fayres' to be written about, where it paid to associate the correct stallholder's name with each stall.

The evangelistic revivals could be quite entertaining if somewhat unsettling owing to long prayers and frequent shouts of 'Hallelujah!'

The local Council meetings were in no way less dramatic than the ones his father had attended in London, and made excellent copy.

During the first couple of years, Ron's daily routine never varied: He would start Monday morning by copying out the tide-tables for the local anglers and add six jokes from a book of funny stories.

At eleven o'clock, the Petty Sessions opened, after which Ron would rush back to the office to transcribe his notes.

He then covered the old kitchen table with a clean sheet of brown paper, which he held down with drawing pins. This was serving him as a memo during that particular week. He would paste everything on to that brown paper that he meant to include in the week's edition of the *Chronicle* until the deadline at five-thirty on Friday afternoon.

Ron preferred to spend Monday afternoons quietly writing up the Court column and maybe a wedding in advance or he would visit a bereaved family, but more often than not, this was interrupted by urgent assignments. By then, he had still eight pages to fill.

On Tuesdays, he was preparing himself for any eventualities and was quite willing to lend a hand at major incidents in town. This would give him a chance to get closer to the people involved, bystanders or policemen, who would then talk more freely, in the hope that a favourable article about their handling of the incident might increase their chances of promotion.

Wednesdays were busy days, because they were tradesmen's days for extra-commercial activities and again, it was important to note down names correctly. Ron loved particularly the amateur stage productions because he could expect complementary tickets to what usually promised to be an entertaining evening. All he needed to do was to compose a piece of critic afterwards, favourably, as the local thespians hoped.

Thursdays were district days, during which he collected local news on a smaller scale, which was often provided in exchange for a beer or nothing at all.

By Friday, the proofs piled up and towards noon, the office became frantic. Five-thirty was the absolute deadline for printing. The flatbed was only halted once in all those years, when the local cinema burnt down – inconsiderately – on a Friday evening.

Ron supplemented his income from the *Chronicle* sometimes by telephoning news from the Exmouth area through to the big papers in London. However, he learnt quickly that they were not quite as scrupulous in re-telling facts, if they had a choice between the truth and a spectacular headline or saucy story. They did not have to live with the consequences which a small town reporter faced when furious readers pointed out misrepresentation and demanded correction.

After about a year as a reporter, Ron began to write a column to which he gave the title *In Town This Week*. This gave him the opportunity to interview famous visitors to the area. Among them were Mantovani, composer and master of a special kind of big band sound; Maurice Chevalier, the French singer and entertainer; Noel Coward, without his searing wit, but with greatly civilised manners; Walt Disney, whom he found disappointingly uninspiring; John Gielgud, a very modest and unassuming man, but immensely interesting to listen to; sports legends like Don Bradman and George Formby; the actresses Jessie Matthews and Gladys Cooper; and Clement Atlee, one time prime minister.

Perhaps the most rewarding interview had been given by George Bernard Shaw, who rarely gave reporters a chance, but who – to everyone's great surprise – invited Ron to question him while spending a holiday in Exmouth. He proceeded to treat Ron like the most acclaimed journalist in the world and was very kind-hearted. Just before leaving Exmouth, Shaw sent Ron one of his famous postcards:

Dear Mr. Delderfield,
I leave tomorrow. The interview was excellent. Few are.
   Many thanks.
                    George Bernard Shaw

However interesting, exciting and varied Ron's job at the *Chronicle* was, Ron felt a little small town claustrophobia creeping in. He couldn't really do much about it, and he was well aware that, having left school without any mentionable qualifications, he did not have much choice and prospects elsewhere. After all, there were seven hundred unemployed at that time in Exmouth among a population of only thirteen thousand five hundred.

Encouraged by the success story of the author Sheriff, who had written *Journey's End*, Ron was convinced that, to make his mark in the world, he had to tread a similar path.

From the age of eighteen, Ron spent most of his free time writing plays and sending them off in large, buff envelopes. His first play – not counting his first attempt at West Buckland School named *Murder in the Pulpit* – had been inspired by a set of cigarette cards called 'Famous Escapes'. The play carried the title *One More Bed*. Its subject was the escape of Napoleonic prisoners from Pembroke jail with the added complication that the one, under whose bed they dug the tunnel, was the traitor.

Ron had the support of Win Davenport, a struggling typist, who sometimes worked for the *Chronicle* and who typed all his scripts at minimal charge or no charge at all. When *One More Bed* was ready to bring Ron fame and fortune, he did not quite know what to do with it. So he contacted his old school friend, Vic Whitworth, who was now working in a London bank, but had not lost his enthusiasm for literature and the theatre. He offered to present Ron's play to a Miss Nancy Price, the founder of the National People's Theatre at the Duchess in Catherine Street. The result was a lot of muttered encouragement for several months, after which nothing more was heard of it.

Ron's next piece of work written in his spare time was a comedy called *The Windfall.*
   It was the story of a Camberwell family who had won a prize at the Irish Sweepstake. When it was just finished, Ron met by chance

27

the actor Walter 'Dickie' Hudd, who agreed to read it. Dickie worked at the London Lighthouse on Hampstead Hill and agreed to become Ron's impresario for the London stage.

However, the bulk of his time was taken up by creasing, reporting and editing for his father's newspaper. His starting salary had been thirty shillings per week, from which five were deducted for his keep.

Soon his father opted more or less out, transferring the paper to Ron and Eric, who re-organised the set-up straight away. Eric was in charge of adverts and layout while Ron remained editor, subeditor and reporter all in one. His new patch comprised parts of East Devon up to the river Exe in the West, to the river Otter in the East and as far as Topsham in the North, all in all about thirty-six square miles. At first, he covered the area by bicycle until he could persuade his father to invest £20 in an Austin Seven touring model.

Around the same time, Ron discovered Carlyle's *French Revolution* which was written like an eye-witness account of the chaotic and terrible happenings in France between 1789 and 1795. This and Lockart's The Life of Napoleon inspired him to read voraciously about this era and to write a series of disconnected episodes called *The Adventures of Cornet Cavendish.*

When not writing in his spare time, Ron indulged in his other passion, the cinema. The 'talkies' had arrived in Exmouth in the winter of 1929/30 and Ron was fascinated.

In summer 1930, Ron went with his brother Eric by train to Wales to have a holiday. In one of the youth hostels, where they stayed overnight, they joined a group of young Northerners, among them two girls. One did all the talking while the other seemed shy and demure. Ron having always had a weakness for demure young ladies fell for it again, this time rather seriously. He was smitten by 'her fresh boyish face, with a long jaw line and high cheek-bones that cast deep shadows under blue eyes. Her shingled hair was dark chestnut, cut in a straight, bewitching fringe…which gave her a touch of medieval glamour.' In spite of being dressed in a pretty chiffon frock, she created a pageboy impression and he noticed her beautiful hands with long, tapering fingers.

On the evening of the day they had first met, he managed to smuggle himself next to her in a concert ticket queue. They developed quickly an easy relationship and were the butt of jokes from the rest of the group because they became inseparable and managed frequently to get conveniently lost on group excursions.

Maimie – everybody seemed to call her by that name – came from South Manchester and worked as a microscopist for a firm engaged in producing university slides. She had lost her mother when she had been nine and lived with her father and step-mother. She had a sister who was married to a university professor, had two small children and lived in Cheshire.

Ron felt incredibly comfortable in Maimie's company. For the first time in his life, he did not trouble himself to impress the girl and he was astonished to find that she was terribly sensible and not overly emotional. Their farewell after that week was unsentimental and he had no idea whether he would ever see her again.

On his return, he clubbed together with two pals, Bob Gough and Ken 'Pro' Coombes, to buy an old, shabby caravan, which they renovated and used as a retreat from their parents. There they spent most of their leisure time in the idyllic setting on top of the cliff at Sandy Bay, unsupervised, inviting old school friends like Kay Gibbons, Arthur 'Slippy' Islip and Queenie Greenaway to prepare tea, sausages and beans cooked over a camp fire.

They also dreamt up various schemes to earn extra money. At first, they formed an amateur dramatic society and performed one of Ron's early plays, *An Eye for an Eye*, which entailed a lot of work without much reward. The most successful idea was the foundation of a music group called 'The Octave', in which Ron strummed the ukelele to the accompaniment from the others. They toured the neighbouring villages with their programme and were usually very welcome, with one exception, when the local vicar, clearly not amused, walked out when Ron and 'Pro' sang: 'Why build a wall around a churchyard when nobody wants to get in.'

'The Octave' and their assorted instruments were transported from gig to gig in Ron's little Austin Seven. Afterwards they drove back to Exmouth in high spirits. One memorable evening, Kay felt particularly hemmed in at the back of the car. A box dug terribly into her ribs and she decided to get rid of it. With the carelessness of youth, she scooped the contents out of the box and threw them out of the open windows. Only on the following day did she learn that she had relieved the car of a consignment of starched white collars, which had been destined for Mrs. Delderfield's shop.

Ron loved 'The Octave'– not only did it bring in a bob or two, but it was also a distraction from the daily tedium at the *Chronicle*.

Ron had not heard from Maimie for nearly a year. He spent his next summer holidays in the caravan, feeling a little lonely and depressed owing to the incessant rain. Listlessly, he began to write an Elizabethan adventure.

When he returned home to his parents' house, a surprise awaited him: Maimie had written to enquire where she might buy one of his books. It must have been his brother Eric who had exaggerated Ron's prospects of publication. Nevertheless, Ron was excited to hear from her and replied immediately. He owned up, but sent her most of his scripts to prove that he really was an aspiring author, just not yet a published one.

Maimie responded by giving him attention, fair criticism and the encouragement nobody else dared to give him.

'Up to now, a small group of people had been prepared to accept my claims of possessing genius, but so far none of them had been young and pretty. Maimie was both and extraordinary good company to boot,' he explained.

A year after they had re-established contact, Maimie came to visit a friend in Devon, which gave Ron the chance to take up their friendship where they had left off twelve months before.

This was followed by a long-distance courtship, during which they managed to write 1,400 letters to each other. They met about four or five times per year, often halfway in London, where they acquired blisters walking the pavements and where they drank hundreds of cups of tea at Lyons.

Often they were searching desperately for a quiet, private corner, but only found it once in a niche in the Bloody Tower.

That first Christmas, they strolled through the streets of London, and having missed the last tram, they walked back to the hotel in the freezing cold. There they ordered wine and sandwiches and when they felt suitably restored, Ron surprised Maimie by proposing.

It took another six months until he could afford a ring, which they chose from Liberty's, a sapphire on a diamond chipping base.

He finally put it on Maimie's finger at Battle Abbey in Hastings, 'a suitable place for a writer of historical fiction,' he thought.

A little later in their courtship, they spent a holiday together in the Lake District and another in North Wales. When separation loomed, because they had run out of money, they betted on horses to replenish their funds. That way, they could spend another week together.

Meanwhile, Ron's parents had been on a trip to visit their eldest son Bill in Australia. They had extended their journey to include half the world's countries.

When Ron announced his engagement on their return, they were delighted and rather relieved that Ron had plans to settle down. They had heard rumours about 'goings-on' at the caravan and weren't sure whether they should take them seriously or not. In any case, they were very willing to increase Ron's salary to ensure he would be able to afford postage and train fares to rendez-vous in London or to Manchester where Maimie lived.

The couple only managed hurried meetings every two or three months, always trying to catch the cheapest possible way of travelling, so that they would have a little sum to spend when they met. For the rest of the time, they had to be content with writing to each other, which they did almost daily.

Ron felt inspired. He had a future wife to think of and was determined to succeed.

He began by writing a play about Pontius Pilate titled *Spark in Judea*, which dug deeper into the reasons why Pontius Pilate went to great lengths to avoid handing Jesus over to his enemies.

Ron made also an attempt at an autobiography for a competition and continued to write advertisements for Rowntree's chocolates.

Unfortunately, none of it caught the eye of anyone important. He finally bought himself an *Artists' and Writers' Year Book* and decided to entrust his work to an agent. He chose one at random; it turned out to be Dorothy Allen of 32 Shaftsbury Avenue and her assistant Margery Vosper. The two ladies took him seriously and encouraged him to write a comedy. Shortly afterwards, he submitted *Twilight Call*, the story of an old, lazy Australian and his daughter, who try to sell their pub to an unsuspecting young man.

Writing was done in his bedroom in a new, detached house called The Croft in Exmouth's Gussiford Lane, where his parents had moved to from the flat above the shop. The problem with his new room was its size; he had the choice as to which side of his body he wanted sizzled by the electric heater. The other side would remain frozen unless he swung his typewriter round at certain intervals.

It was time to fly the nest!

In spring 1932, Ron sealed his future with the demurest of them all and married Maimie in the All Saints' Registry Office in Manchester. His bride wore a leaf-green two-piece suit and hat with a brown-spotted eye-veil. Attending were his parents, her father and step-mother, Bob Gough from the caravan, Vic Withworth, his old school friend from 'The Grange', who now worked in a London bank, Robin, his new sister-in-law, who provided the wedding breakfast at her home outside Altrincham, and her husband and their children.

Two nights before the wedding, Ron had wrecked the Austin Seven and injured himself in the process, so that the bridegroom turned up with an enormous plaster across the bridge of his swollen nose.

Ron was quite shocked how quickly the ceremony was over. When the young couple found themselves in a taxi which took them to Altrincham, they were both tongue-tied with embarrassment. When Ron finally found his voice again, he addressed his young wife – for no apparent reason and for the rest of his life – by her proper name, May.

They spent a hectic honeymoon, visiting his six aunts who still lived in London and his favourite uncle who worked for Lloyds. For the rest of the time, they went sightseeing, visited the theatre every night and rummaged around in antique markets. May seemed to have an innate ability to find genuine antiques at bargain prices, and surprised her new husband by purchasing a stained and badly-dented tankard with an ornamental handle for four-and-sixpence, which she sold some time later for £5.

May had also very particular ideas about furnishing her new home in Exmouth. If it had been for her, she would have filled the three-bedroomed, detached house called 'Leonora', which they rented, with antiques and second-hand furniture. However, Ron felt rather uneasy, if not embarrassed, about installing his young wife among other people's cast-offs.

They found a compromise in buying two well-made suites from a respectable firm in Tottenham Court Road with the £200 that he had saved during the preceding four years in the red money-box that, in childhood, he had shared with his brother Eric. It still baffled him, why his parents and his brothers had been constantly amused by his careful book-keeping of pocket money and earnings.

Even with the most stringent economies, managing married life on his income was not easy. Ron kept on writing and submitting plays, but received about five rejection slips per week. May had the brilliant idea of accommodating holiday-makers. Since the little house in one of the new roads behind Exmouth was too small for this enterprise, they moved across the road to a four-bedroomed house with lattice windows and the name 'Oak Park'. In the smallest of the bedrooms, Ron put his desk and typewriter and began to write about what he knew best, the world of small town journalism. The play was called *Fleet Street in Lilliput*. It would be staged one day under the title *Printer's Devil* and turned into the novel *All Over the Town*.

Meanwhile, the basic income was provided by Ron's work as a reporter, editor and sub-editor at the *Exmouth Chronicle* and May's paying holiday guests. She also haunted auction houses for bargains, which she stored in the box-like drawing room and sold on whenever possible.

They lived on £5 a week, from which they had to pay twenty-two and sixpence for rent and nine shillings for rates. Any luxuries, like a meal out or a visit to the cinema, were financed by selling off unwanted wedding gifts.

May was not only enormously supportive of her husband's writing, but also shared his love for the cinema and a sense of humour. He discovered her charming habit of talking through her laughter and found her unshakeable loyalty very reassuring in times when constant rejection of his plays cast a shadow over both their hopes of future success and threatened to undermine his self-confidence.

In 1937, *Spark in Judea* was performed on a Sunday night at the Ambassador Theatre in London's West End but was forgotten soon afterwards.

At the end of November 1937, Ron met an actor of a touring company strolling along the beach in Exmouth. They got talking and, among other things, Ron mentioned his play *Twilight Call*. When the actor asked to see the script, Ron realised that his only copy had been sent to the Birmingham Repertory Theatre two years earlier, and had never been heard of since.

Ron decided to ask for it back, and was most astonished to receive a telegram by return, saying: 'Don't ask for it back now, we are doing it next week!' Ron mistrusted his good fortunes and travelled immediately to Birmingham. There, for the first time in his life, he found his name on a hoarding, which was immensely flattering.

However, after a fortnight's performance, the play sunk back into oblivion; Ron had reached the end of another cul-de-sac.

The 'Q' Theatre made an attempt at staging *Printer's Devil* a few months later.

After a week at the 'Q', the play was transferred to the Embassy Theatre in Swiss Cottage, where it received much improved reviews. The play moved then to Northampton and to the Civic repertory Theatre in Bradford.

Ron brushed these experiences aside, as he had something much more important to occupy his mind: May was expecting their first child. They were delighted and didn't worry unduly, when they were told fairly early on that May would have to have a Caesarean operation. They knew it would be quite expensive, but Ron begged his old friend, the poet John Pudney, who presented a series on the radio called *Fact Or Fiction*, to lobby on his behalf.

The result was a commission to write a play on mermaids for a half-an-hour's broadcast – not that Ron was any authority on the subject! This introduced him to Felix Felton, who worked at the West Regional Headquarters of the BBC, who in turn asked him to write a few comedy scripts about a small-town newspaper. It was the birth of the very popular radio series *The Cocklemouth Comet*. It featured various local events each fortnight.

Ron was pleased; he seemed to have progressed professionally, but privately, he and May were very unhappy, because their first child was still-born. May recovered physically rather quickly, but, of course, they both felt an enormous sense of loss and were very upset.

Up to this point in 1939, Ron had written fifteen plays, of which four had been actually staged by the Birmingham Repertory and the 'Q' Theatre in London. He had also written five novels, a countless number of short stories – all unpublished – and many short plays for the local amateur dramatic societies. Moreover, he had edited some four hundred and fifty editions of the *Exmouth Chronicle*, from which he drew his sole steady income. His net profit as an author had been negligible, amounting to only twenty-five pounds.

Ron also had an offer of eight hundred pounds for the film rights of *Printer's Devil*, but then history put a spoke in his career wheel: the Hitler–Stalin pact was signed in August and on September 3rd all theatres closed.

Ron was not really a political person. He had tried out various convictions: as a teenager, he had been a conformist, turning to communism, then militant pacifism, graduating at twenty-four to be a staid Liberal. He had signed the Canon Dick Sheppard's Peace Pledge, but had demanded his card back after Munich. He had followed developments on the continent with his usual professional interest and had been rattled, when in spring 1938, he had met a Jew on a short holiday to Exmouth, who had said wistfully that, 'he was living on borrowed time and that that man will come for us soon.'

Ron had kept in contact with this man, but after the summer of Munich, he never heard from him again. Ron had shared the general relief when Chamberlain had stepped down from the plane, 'smiling his rabbit-toothed smile and waving his famous piece of paper,' but it failed to reassure him and he rather feared that the roof would fall in on everyone sooner or later.

Ron carried on running the *Chronicle* and sending off manuscripts to publishers, theatre managements, actors and whoever promised to advance his writing career.

May was expecting their second child, but again heartbreak awaited them; that January, their second baby was still-born, leaving May terribly ill. She did recover eventually, at least physically. The emotional scars took a lot longer to heal.

THREE

New Beginnings
(1954)

It is January 1st, 1956, a grey and stormy winter's morning. The winds are howling around Lower Coombe and through the tree tops in the garden. Ronald Frederick Delderfield feels snug in his study on the ground floor, his most favourite place in the world. He sits at his desk, a wall of books behind him, his old typewriter in front of him and the obligatory cup of strong, black coffee beside it. He shivers a little looking through the window at nature's mayhem outside, but wrenches his eyes immediately away, because he is on an important mission.

He is nearly forty-four years of age, a tall figure with broad shoulders and a little extra weight round his midriff. The half-circle of fine brown hair above the back of his neck underlines the complete baldness atop. Sparkling, combative blue eyes lurk behind thick dark-rimmed glasses and the cigarette between nicotine-stained fingers indicates that he is ready for battle.

He can hear his wife May bustling with household chores. Occasionally the high pitched, excited voices of their two children, Veronica and Paul, drift to the study, followed immediately by admonishing words of their mother who will not have father disturbed.

Ron smiles thinking of May. He doubts that he would have had the courage to reinvent himself as a full-time novelist without his wife's loyal support and unstinting faith in his talent as a writer. He is a very lucky man indeed!

They are both aware that there will be a considerable drop in income during his first year as a novelist. They have moved to a smaller Devon cottage in Tipton St. John in anticipation. The royalties of his most famous theatre play *Worm's Eye View* and the salary earned as a journalist on his father's newspaper, the *Exmouth Chronicle*, had given them a comfortable lifestyle in the past ten years which they will now have to relinquish – they hope only for a short while. When they decided that he should concentrate on writing novels, May joked that she could easily go back to taking in lodgers or expand her small antiques business if things didn't work out. She knows that Ron's great love has always been storytelling. He truly believes that the heart of it can only be found between hardback covers. Now he has committed himself to producing stories which will delight and captivate his readers.

Ron shudders at the thought of the theatre world, how he had worked for years 'cheek by jowl with talkative madmen who threatened to throw themselves off Westminster Bridge' whenever he insisted that they stick to his text.

At first, he was exhilarated by his West End success, but the thrill had worn off quickly. He has never understood theatrical temperaments and erratic flamboyant natures. He is a West Country man, down to earth, outspoken and passionate about England, its history and traditions, his family and young people in general. He hates political correctness and pretentiousness of any kind. The complicated world of West End Theatres left him often baffled and exasperated. He is much more at home in his study, surrounded by books, knowing his family nearby, free to let his imagination roam, writing what he has always wanted to write and not what fashion dictates.

Ron brushes his hand over his forehead as if to sweep unpleasant memories away. With an enormous sense of liberation, he begins to type. He has decided to write the story of an Avenue and its people. He intends to describe the everyday flow of life for the Avenue families, each reflecting some special aspect of the nineteen-twenties and thirties. Ron is in his element. He sets about to entertain himself and his readers. Turning to romance and history, two of his favourite topics, is a wonderful relief after the frenzied struggle with the precise demands of comedy laughter.

He has already drawn up a plan of his imaginary Avenue and its inhabitants: his main character is Jim Carver, a Socialist, who is involved in the General strike of 1926. Then there is Archie Carver, an ex-errand boy and backstreet Don Juan, who becomes a black marketer with a chain of grocery shops; Edith Clegg lives at No.3, a spinster who plays romantic accompaniments to the epics of Rudolph Valentino when she doesn't have to care for a sister, who has gone mildly peculiar over an earlier love affair. Elaine Frith of No.17 is scheming to break out of her stuffy family circle and to find The Great Provider who will worship her, body and soul; Esme Fraser is besotted with Elaine, but is in for a big disappointment until he finds Judy Carver, who has always shared his dreams; the daredevil temperaments of the terrible twins, Boxer and Bernard are finally channelled by Commando actions on the battlefields; Ted Hartnell, the jazz drummer and his wife Margy have their efforts to build him up to a big-band leader undermined by the war; and Harold Godber, the rallying point of Avenue bowler hats, woos and weds the pretty widow at No.22, and ultimately, his nerve broken by the Luftwaffe, finds new courage in the unlikely friendship with a neighbour he has always regarded as a Bolshie.

These are the people Ron will live with every day for the next year. He will share their trials and tribulations until the two volumes, *The Dreaming Suburb* and *The Avenue Goes to War*, have been finished. Out of Ron's pen pour the characters and their stories against the backdrop of political as well as social upheaval between the end of the First World War up to the arrival of Hitler's air fleet over the terraced houses (1919 to 1940) and, in the second tome, through the war years until the survivors pick up the pieces, count their blessings and carry on with their lives (1940 to 1947).

There is a knock on the door. May comes in with a fresh cup of coffee.

'How is it going?' she smiles.

It is a momentous day for both of them. From now on, he will be at home most days to write like 'the blazes', three hours in the morning and two hours before supper, seven days a week. No more hurried and futile trips from Devon to London to meet with theatre producers, directors or actors. He will only make an exception for his agent Felix de Wolfe. Ronnie Delderfield, the playwright is in the past; R.F. Delderfield, the novelist, has been born.

'I shall write a straight forward story of a group of undistinguished British people,' he hesitates, mulls it over and grins apologetically: 'the only kind of people I really know'.

May sees the passion in his eyes and nods in agreement.

FOUR

The original Avenue
(1918 – 1923)

Ron knew Avenue life well.

During the years of the First World War, Ron, his parents and older brother Eric had frequently visited relatives in Penshurst and Leigh in Kent, to have a break from the dangers of war-torn London. They had found it increasingly difficult to return to Bermondsey, where they lived, and to leave the tranquillity of the countryside for the Inner City. Mr. Delderfield senior would probably have stayed in London, as did most of his six sisters, who all lived in the vicinity of Tower Bridge, but the air-raids took their toll on Mrs. Delderfield's nerves. Ron nearly choked with excitement when he was told in the early spring of 1918, that they were moving to the country for good.

William James Delderfield, moved his wife Alice and his two youngest sons Eric and Ron – the eldest, William, had run away and by then joined the Merchant Navy – out of the range of the London air raids, to the then rural Addiscombe on the Kent/Surrey border, where an uncle of the boys had recently bought a house in Ashburton Avenue. Addiscombe was then a suburb of Croydon which grew between the Lower and Upper Addiscombe Road within sight of the old Shirley Mill and the seemingly vast and untouched expanse of the Shirley Hills.

The Delderfields settled at No. 22, a 'good class' detached residence, a little set back from the road. It was a genteel neighbourhood, which ran on the rules of conventionality and formality, which had been utterly lacking in London. It had a mellow air and thrived on the consciousness of its residents that they had a great deal in common and an obligation to conform. In fact, the Avenue dwellers revelled in it and everyone knew their place; it was a community safe and ordered.

Ashburton Avenue was only five minutes walk from the ruins of the old military academy set up by the East India Company, a haven for the boys to roam.

On the 11th November that year, little Ron and his mother took

39

a bus to Croydon High Street to wave excitedly a sixpenny Union Jack to celebrate the end of the First World War. He did not quite understand what the excitement was all about, but he was swept up in the general mood of joy, relief and happiness.It never occurred to the family to move back to London now that hostilities had ended.

Mr. Delderfield led a hectic life. His train journey to Smithfield's Market in London – where he continued to work as a buyer, travelling to farms to select cattle – was now even more time consuming. He took the South-Eastern and Chatham commuter line, beginning daily at 3.40 a.m. (because he came from Addiscombe; he got up at 4 a.m. when he lived in London) from Woodside station. He had to give up his political ambitions at the Bermondsey Council, where he had been known as a fiery speaker. However, he replaced them immediately with the Addiscombe P.S.A., which stood for Pleasant Sunday Afternoon, a gathering of members from the local Baptist chapel congregation.

Avenue Sundays were a trial for Mrs. Delderfield. At ten o'clock in the morning the Sabbath panic was well under way. Mr. Delderfield took the boys to Chapel, but they always arrived late, not least because the children were very reluctant to accompany father, in fear that he would make them render the 'dear children's hymn.' Ron hated the regimented services and compared them later to that of a well run prison. While father and sons attended church, Mrs. Delderfield battled with Sunday lunch for the family and with the preparations for the afternoon guests.

She had never taken well to the life of a housewife, mother and hostess. Before marriage, she had been a live-in shop assistant in a London drapery business and was dedicated to money-making. Household chores bored her to tears and she performed her duties with scant grace. Cooking Sunday lunch and entertaining guests for the rest of the day was not her idea of a pleasant Sunday. But there was little she could do to stop her zealous husband. Her boys, Ron and Eric, did not look forward to these meetings either as they had to spend the rest of the Sunday in their best clothes being paraded before the members of the P.S.A.

Ron's intellectual and spiritual home life was more dramatic than that of most other children because his family was divided down the middle. His mother was stubbornly High Tory while her husband remained a fiery Radical throughout his life. To Ron this was nothing new; theirs had always been a chaotic, noisy and volatile household.

Mrs. Delderfield was an unemotional mother, but she was keen to instil good manners and discipline in her children. It was important to her that the boys did not let her down in public and that she was considered highly by her neighbours. The quiet avenue provided peace and tranquillity for her nerves shattered by the constant attacks on war-time London, but to her it meant also advancement in society.

Ron loved to escape to his new surroundings and adored the personal freedom they brought him: lying in the long meadow grass in the Shirley Hills by the Old Mill, breathing fresh country air and listening to bird song – this was his kind of heaven, a butterfly moment!

When not out in the hills, Ron played with his brother Eric. They had been warned not to roam the streets with village louts, so they enlisted Sidney Brommet, the son of their next door neighbour, for their games. He was a well-behaved, timid boy who soon became a victim of the boisterous Delderfield brothers. Their playground was a derelict lot adjoining their backyard where they played rumbustious games which left poor Sydney often in tears.

One hot June evening, they hit upon the unfortunate idea to use a chamber pot as a soldier's helmet for Sydney's head. It got promptly stuck. Avoiding their parents' wrath, they tried for an hour to free their long-suffering friend, who by then couldn't stop sobbing. In the end, they had to admit defeat and formed a sorry procession for home and help. Mrs. Delderfield marched them down to the local hospital where it took another few hours and plenty of liquid soap to prise the pot gently and safely from the quivering lad.

Ron's sense of adventure led him to another interest. He threw himself with tremendous gusto into emulating Robinson Crusoe. He was determined to build a seaworthy raft. His first unsuccessful attempt was on a railway sleeper upon the golf-links pond at Addiscombe. This wouldn't carry him at all. Next he thought of a construction of wooden boxes nailed together with laths. He enlisted two friends to help him carry the contraption the three miles to Ham Farm Pond in the Elmers End district. That, too, ended in failure, when Ron nearly drowned and, to his mother's fury, ruined a good shirt in the process. He was subsequently banned from leaving the garden for the rest of the holiday.

Ron turned, out of necessity and boredom, to reading. He engrossed himself in youth magazines like *B.O.P.* with its highly adventurous historical fiction, *My Magazine* by Arthur Mee, which was more factual, *Rainbow*, *Puck* – the adventures at a boarding school – and *Chum*, whose author, Walkey, greatly influenced young Ron's mind.

The publishing event of the week, however, were *The Magnet* and *The Gem*, both featuring school stories, and *The Boy's Friend*, dealing with the adventures of Jimmy Oliver and his two companions.

During his life in the Avenue, Ron discovered the cinema, a hobby, which would become a lifelong passion. He learnt to be very adept at escaping his mother's clutches and at sneaking off to the Scala cinema in Croydon's High Street. There he saw Matheson Lang in *Dick Turpin*, *Lorna Doone*, *Orphans of the Storm* and Douglas Fairbanks in *The Black Pirate* and *Robin Hood*.

Ron's mind was like a sponge when it came to adventure, romance and history. He loved the heroes, who fought against all the odds to victory; who defended their personal freedom against narrow-mindedness and convention and the happy endings appealed greatly to his romantic nature. The films were a constant source of fascination and escapism and no effort of his mother to curb his appetite for screen adventure could stop him.

Ron managed to mollify her by agreeing to undertake piano lessons as was fashion among the avenue children. His first teacher was a sweet little spinster called Mrs. Dixon, who made him learn the obligatory pieces of *Down on the Farm*, *In a Quiet Wood*, *The March of the Farmers' Men* and, of course, the ever present *The Merry Peasant Returning from Work*. His mother thought him exceptionally gifted and pinned her hopes on his becoming a second Rubinstein, but subsequently another tutor was more ruthless in informing her that she had grossly overestimated his chances of playing at the Albert Hall. To the day she died, she believed that the world had been deprived of a musical genius, because once the gramophone had taken over and replaced the piano, Ron never played again.

Eric and Ron were first sent to a gentecl private primary school, The South London New College, whose headmaster, Mr. Scobie, impressed the boys with his natty attire. There were a hundred and fifty pupils, on whose purple and white caps was emblazoned 'S.N.C.' which earned them the local soubriquet Scobie's Nannygoats

Collection. In spite of this being a very pretentious establishment, none of the staff were properly qualified and their disciplinary powers were frequently insufficient.

Ron's first experience of secondary education was an unfortunate one. He was packed off to Lucknow Park School, a Board School, which no 'nice' boys in the avenue attended. It was like a huge lavatory, with half-tiled walls, varnished partitions and goal-like railing enclosures.

Ron made no friends and was terrified of the headmaster, who liberally distributed lashings with the cane. Academically, Ron could hold his own, as the intelligence quotient of the class was very low, but this did not soften the blow of a ghastly experience. The only pleasant memory he took away, was his introduction to Tennyson's poetry, *The Lady of Shalott* and *Silas Marner*.

During his time at Lucknow Park School, it was found that Ron had a 'wonky eye'. Glasses were prescribed and after a month or two he could not do without them. This underlined his owlish appearance and made him the butt of jokes and as a result, he tried to keep an even lower profile than before.

When Mrs. Delderfield realised with what kind of boys he was sharing his desk, she applied to send him to Selhurst Grammar. Ron had to pass an oral examination and when he did so with ease, his father was so impressed by his erudition that he took him on impulse on a historical tour of the Chislehurst Caves as a reward. It was the first time that Ron had known his father to be proud of him, and had acknowledged him as a possible embryo student of his hero Abraham Lincoln.

Unfortunately, Eric, Ron's older brother, who had joined Selhurst Grammar before him, had not made an entirely favourable impression. He was constantly in and out of trouble at the school and at home, because he treated schoolmasters with contempt and had a mutinous spirit. Most of his teachers had written him off, but, as so often happens, after he left school, he applied himself to work with unremitting vigour, first as a printing apprentice and later in the family business.

Understandably, the teachers at Selhurst Grammar were at first sceptical about another member of the Delderfield family joining the school, but Ron was a subdued little boy who did what he was told and seemed rather fearful.

The legacy of the horrors of Lucknow Park school was that Ron showed a marked inclination for morbidity. His favourite poem became *Tommy's Prayer*, and his favourite occupation was to walk up to Shirley churchyard and read the inscriptions on the tombstones. He spent many solitary hours in the glades of the Wickham Woods and developed an inexplicable fixation on the possibilities of being buried alive unless he performed certain self-imposed tasks. These were numerous, onerous and grew in number by the day. They were in the realms of abject confessions to his mother of practically every waking thought, or of not stepping on lines of flagstones, or of playing the tune, he was practising on the piano, three times without making a mistake. He worked himself into a pitiful state and began to sleep very badly; he became indifferent to punishment or reward, stopped enjoying the mellow surroundings of the Addiscombe scenery, and prayed for death in any shape or form. He was kept prisoner by obsession and – as his family called it – 'Ron's Little Voices'.

It took him months to pull himself out of this depressive mood which was a natural reaction to a period of extreme physical repression. But one fine spring morning in 1920, another little voice defeated all others by telling him to look forward to the Easter Holidays as other children did. He suddenly realised, that nobody would be buried alive, however wicked they might be, never mind failing to play *Lead Kindly Light* three times faultlessly on the upright. He could not understand, where this voice of reason had suddenly sprung from, but he felt the enormous relief of a burden being lifted and buoyancy returning to his spirit.

The 'Little Voices' did not surrender altogether, but reared their heads for years to come and left a mark on Ron as the most vivid experience of his life, the difference between life and death, sanity and lunacy. It gave him an insight into the fragility of the mind and taught him sensitivity towards the emotions and foibles of fellow human beings.

Ron's elder brother Bill did not live with the family in the Avenue. He was eleven years older than Ron and had run away in 1917 to join the Merchant Navy against his father's will. He was torpedoed on his first day out of harbour and adrift in an open boat before being rescued. Ron remembered him as a sort of Beau Geste figure, who had taught him how to tell the time by the kitchen clock and who had saved him from drowning during one of the family holidays.

The next time Bill turned up, it was as a survivor of a South American convoy.

After demobilisation, he worked as a butcher in Peckham for a year, but that was too humdrum for him and he announced that he would be off again.

On a dank, dark January morning, the family waved him off to Australia. There he stayed, married an Australian girl named Freda, joined the police and finally became Police Commissioner of Tasmania after an Act of Parliament made it possible for him as a foreigner to take up the post. Things happened to Bill as they never happened to the rest of the family. Ron never ceased to admire his eldest brother in spite of not seeing him for thirty-five years.

Ron remembered the Ashburton Avenue throughout his life with great fondness. Suburbia wasn't 'smug, half-cultured and narrow-in-outlook', as the dictionary defines it. To him the avenue was 'full of magic, texture, colour, songs, tragedy and farce'. He could picture 'the trim crescents and closes with their neat privet hedges and tiny front gardens enclosed by dwarf walls and looped chains, their turbaned, industrious housewives scouring the front steps and parlour windows, the tradesmen's vans and whistling errand boys, the snip-snap of the hand-shears and whirr of hand-mowers and always the rendition of *L'Orange* and other pieces coaxed from upright pianos by unlucky wights; the sniff of burning leaves in autumn and of bonfires, on which the children roasted potatoes, slinging them at each other when the adults weren't looking.'

To a child transported from Inner London to the suburb, there was no end of romance, particularly to one with the vivid imagination, inquisitiveness and thirst for adventure of a young Ron Delderfield.

During the summer holidays in 1923, Ron met his first love on school sports day, when he bought an ice cream cone and ended up by giving it to Connie Copplestone. She had fluffy, brown curls, blue eyes and an unbelievably demure expression.

He saw her again on the following day outside a newsagent's where he had gone to buy his comic. She pointed out that his bike had fallen over and invited him to walk her home.

They spent all summer holiday together, sanctioned by his mother, who was glad that he seemed to have given up on his more dangerous pursuits. It was a placid partnership without promises and declarations. Connie, unusually gentle-natured for a ten-year–old, knew how to iron out the stresses of life. He gave her all his cigarette cards and flushed with pride when complimented on his good taste, as if he had been applauded for a spectacular triumph. Connie's demure expression was to define Ron's taste in women and leave him susceptible to it all his life.

The Delderfield's life in the avenue and Ron's first love came to an abrupt end. In late autumn 1923, Ron's father declared that he had bought a business in the West Country and that he was about to uproot the family again.

FIVE

Post- Avenue and *Diana*
(1956 -1959)

For two years Ron is totally involved with his Avenue characters. He writes with irresistible humour, subtly funny, sometimes even saucy but never rude.

He describes poor old Harold Godber, the 'bowler hat' as 'thirty-five and still virginal, longing to grasp something less crackly than a bundle of share certificates and a mortgage deed' and as 'spare, eager, bespectacled and physically frail, but also fussy, pedantic and inclined to be pompous,' a man who finds himself having to deal with 'a woman, whose china-blue eyes and tiny rosebud mouth causes him to stammer every time he begins to speak to her.'

Ron has also great fun in mimicking accents on paper, like Jim Carver's Polish boss, Mr. Sokolski, or old Mr. Piretta, Archie's long suffering Italian father-in-law. In spite of having both lived in England for most of their lives, they have never managed to lose their accents and speak English with the intonation of their mother tongues.

Ron also feels great satisfaction when he can occasionally let one of his strongly held beliefs creep into the story and have it expressed by one of the characters: 'A boy like this would always be at war, if not with the Germans, then with the social conditions into which he had been born; all his life he would be involved in the hopeless fight of the under-privileged against the smug and the well-breeched!'

Exasperation transpires when he writes 'the symptom of the whole rotten system, a system of exploitation and dividends and gold standards, and endless hair-splitting over conference tables'.

Esme, the dreamer of the Avenue story, volunteers for the RAF because he has come to believe that 'defeat by the Germans would be worse than extinction.'

Ron's passionate social conscience always shines through and he sees his writing as an opportunity to defend the weak under-dog: 'Tell us what the Industrial Revolution had made of the people whose grandfathers drifted into the Northern and Midland towns from the farms and cottage looms. Distil for us some of the traditional humour of the Cockney, and the Lancashire people. Find us a latterday Weller or Micawber, THAT's the sort of shot in the arm that English fiction needs today.'

His friends know that he is 'one for the workers', that he will stand up for the disadvantaged and fight with and for them. He will support and amuse the readers of local newspapers with his outspokenness and passion defending the young, traditions, morals and above all, Englishness. Ron believes firmly in the decency of his people and that they are going to win in the end!

'Without this I would cease to believe in anything,' he tells one journalist in an interview and looks him straight in the eye.

The Avenue story does not have a happy ending, but it leaves the reader with a feeling of hope and the confidence that the dreams of ordinary people matter, even if they don't always come true, just like in real life.

For two years, the Avenue characters take over their creator's every waking thought. They tyrannise him and he learns to love them for it. Ron admits later that 'when some were killed in the Blitz it was like losing old friends. One I actually reprieved by tearing up the manuscript and starting the chapter again! They are still more real to me than the people I meet.'

The submission of the two volumes, *The Dreaming Suburb* and *The Avenue Goes to War* is a heart-stopping moment for the Delderfields. May knows how important a breakthrough as a novelist is for her husband. He wants to provide well for the family, to re-capture financial ease of previous years, but he is also passionately committed to writing novels whatever the outcome.

May understands that he needs to shut himself away to create his fictional worlds. Occasionally she worries that he smokes too much, drinks endless cups of coffee, but she is pleased that he has begun to set the afternoons aside for physical exercise like walking, swimming or riding, but most of all, she delights in his enthusiasm and torrent of creative output.

Soon after the publication of the *Avenue* story it becomes clear that the public and critics approve. It is hailed as 'a suburban *War and Peace*' and its author is described as 'a master painter of the mundane'.

The financial rewards are a little disappointing, but Ron works out fairly quickly that making his story adaptable for alternative media will increase his income. When asked by the BBC to write an *Avenue* script for radio, he agrees and spends another year working on the adaptation of both volumes. They begin life on October, 9th 1959 as a radio serial under the title *People Like Us* featuring Jim Norton, Michael Lees, Jennifer Daniel, Miles Anderson and Shirley Cain; the producer is James Brabazon.

People Like Us acquires a devoted audience; they can identify with the characters and their experiences between and during the war years.

Ron needs to move on. Again, he clears his book shelves in his study and fills them with background reading material for his new project. He steeps himself in its surroundings, atmosphere and the history of the time he wants to write about. He continues to write with the methodical approach of a quantity surveyor, 5,000 words each day.

Ron feels enormous relief not having to travel up to London on a fortnightly basis to see through the productions of his plays; twice a year is sufficient.

He also refuses to take holidays; he doesn't feel the need to go abroad. In fact he writes: 'I can never be absent from Britain for more than twelve hours without feeling the pangs of homesickness, and the older I grow, the more mulishly insular I become.'

Protected by May's willingness to keep all household and family problems from him, Ron begins his next canvas, an intense love story of two adolescents before a background of unspoilt East Devon countryside. The plot is simple: fifteen year old Jan Leigh, an orphan, helping his uncle in a second-hand furniture shop in a small Devon seaside resort, falls in love with the only daughter of a wealthy financier, who bought the local manor to play squire. Her name is Diana Gayelord-Sutton. They spin their dreams in the gleaming purple and gold stretch of land, which only they know as Sennacharib. In reality it is called Hayes Wood, just south of Woodbury Common.

The drama of youthful romance matures into adult passion, reaching its climax in war torn France where Jan and Diana meet up again in the Resistance, fighting ultimately not the adults anymore, who had objected to their childish love, but the Nazis who threaten the lovely land of Sennacharib and all it stands for in their eyes

May is sure that the volatile Diana is an identikit of all the gorgeous, heartbreaking actresses her husband has ever met in his previous career as a playwright.

'And hasn't Jan a lot of the young Ron in him?' she muses, 'generous, soft-hearted, passionate, impulsive, out-spoken and tremendously loyal.'

She laughs as she remembers one of Ron's statements: 'happy marriages generally are... just getting on. Well, being romantic, it doesn't stop all of a sudden; it sort of crystallises and gets more comfortable. You get round to preferring a chair each... hang on to all this as long as you can. It only comes once, you know.'

They have become very comfortable with each other and she is going to hang on to this compulsive scribbler for the rest of their lives!

Meanwhile, the Delderfield's have moved two more times, first to Sheldon, the 'wrong' side of the Exe, and then to Wales, but these times away from East Devon are always short-lived. It is East Devon they all love and consider their home.

By 1960 Ron has finished the first of two volumes, *There Was A Fair Maid Dwelling*, followed two years later by the sequel, *The Unjust Skies*.

The success in England is muted, when first published, but when it comes out in the USA under the title *Diana* it becomes the Literary Choice for the month of September. Ron is puzzled and not a little annoyed that his novels about English people and the English countryside should be more appreciated in the States than at home. He loves the story and thinks it deserves better.

'Reading *Diana* nobody would guess that you were born in London', observes May to her husband.

She was brought up in Manchester but feels an equally intense love for the Devon countryside. Neither of them have shed their respective tell-tale accents but they feel accepted and entirely at home in the West Country

'I lived here longer than anywhere else; I was eleven, when I came here,' he explains, 'I remember father telling us that he had bought a business in Exmouth.' Ron shakes his head at the memory of their abrupt departure from the Avenue:

'Mother was rather shocked; she loved living in Addiscombe. The only thing that mollified her was the prospect of having her own business. And then we arrived here just before Christmas 1923, and they lost all my presents during the move.'

SIX

Exmouth and the Grange
(1923 – 1926)

The Delderfield's had outgrown the Addiscombe Avenue. Moreover, Ron's father, William James Delderfield, then fifty years of age, had become restless and disillusioned with his job at Smithfield's market. He was fed up with the daily train journey, starting at 3.40 a.m. every morning from Woodside station, which became particularly uncomfortable in the winter. The break was precipitated when a change in job with a view of a partnership didn't materialise. Shortly afterwards, a neighbour of the Delderfields, who originated from Devon, returned from holiday and reported that he had seen a business going cheap in Exmouth. Mr. Delderfield did not take long to make a snap-decisions: he bought the business and informed his wife and sons that they would move to the South West.

The business comprised printing works, a stationery, wool and toy shop and a weekly local newspaper, all housed in a three-storey building called Berlin House in the main street of Exmouth. Mrs. Delderfield hated being uprooted from the genteel suburban life, but was mollified by the prospect of running the shop and delegating the wretched household chores to a maid.

Mr Delderfield and his second eldest son Eric went the week before Christmas to prepare the arrival of the rest of the family. Ron and his mother followed on Christmas Eve. The partners of the business lived on the first floor, while the Delderfields occupied the top floor. In the general chaos of moving from Surrey to Devon all of Ron's Christmas presents had been mislaid until they were discovered piece by piece around mid-January.

Their new home was a treasure trove. The boys spent weeks exploring it, supervised only superficially by the new maid, called Gert. She was nineteen, sandy-haired and blue-eyed and to the delight of her two unruly charges, absolutely irrepressible. She came from an enormous family of a West Country sea-captain, who had gone down with his ship in a storm. Gert told her family's history with the lovely burr of the West Country dialect which kept Ron enthralled. He never seemed to get enough of her stories about her numerous sisters and her one hundred year old grandmother who lived with them.

Ron was very fond of Gert, who seemed to be solely in charge of him. While doing her chores, she taught him every verse and chorus of every smash-hit between 1923 and 1926. Her favourite was *Felix kept on Walking*. She also taught him to dance the foxtrot and took him to visit her friends in the rural areas behind Exmouth.

Whenever he had a misadventure, she would screen him from authority, and it was she who was responsible for his becoming a *Treasure Island* addict from the age of twelve. She had given him a beautifully illustrated edition for his birthday, which he read aloud to her as she went about her duties. Around the same time, he discovered *Huckleberry Finn* which he found absolutely fascinating. He re-read both copies so often that they soon fell to bits; but they remained his most favourite copies for the rest of his life.

Ron teamed up with Tiny, one of Gert's family, who was as dedicated a worshipper of the screen as Ron was. Gert used to give him sixpence for the cinema on the condition that he would return the favour to her with a blow-by-blow account of each film afterwards.

The move to Exmouth, twelve miles south of Exeter, had been an astounding piece of good fortune as far as his passion for the cinema was concerned, because it multiplied his choice of 'cathedrals' by four, and that – in 1923 – in a town of eleven thousand inhabitants! It only cost sixpence to see shows from six to eleven p.m.. No one could have shown more ingenuity than young Ron to stave off bankruptcy and to pretend to fit in homework and piano practice. He covered his traces with the help of new won friends and often managed to confuse his mother who always tried but rarely succeeded in hauling him out of the movie hall. She finally issued an edict that he was to see one cinema show per week which was the start of a non-stop game of cat and mouse.

The boys saw more of Gert, the maid and home-help, than they did of their parents, who ran the printing press, local newspaper and the shop. Ron seemed prone to accidents and mishaps, often because he was preoccupied with his own dreams and ill thought-through adventures. He considered errands and responsibility transferred to him by his father a nuisance, something to be got rid of quickly, without thinking of the consequences. On one occasion, his father's payment demands, which Ron was supposed to deliver to customers, who were behind settling their bills, happened to float down the river Exe towards Topsham. Admittedly, this had been a task Mr. Delderfield senior had found too embarrassing to execute himself, but he was thoroughly annoyed with his son, when some of the bills had been washed ashore and brought back to him.

Ron ended his eleventh birthday in disgrace, after he and his birthday guest had used the drawing room sofa as a trampoline and left it bereft of springs.

Ron was a sociable lad and made friends quickly. The one with the most disastrous effect on him was undoubtedly Cyril Chown, the son of the local outfitter.

In spite of a strict upbringing by a Sunday school teacher mother and an amateur archaeologist father, nothing could daunt, defeat or depress Cyril. He found an ally in Ron and the two embarked on one adventure after another. The consequences were often painful, not least to Cyril's pale, peaky-looking and bespectacled friend Ron from London. Cyril was a sort of deluxe Huckleberry Finn, and most children in Exmouth were barred from socialising with him. Ron was not among them and together they put some of the most outrageous and dangerous ideas into execution. They cut up pillows, scattering their contents into the street shouting: 'It's snowing!' Or they lay on the Delderfield's flat roof, shooting peas at prospective customers, until Mr. Delderfield senior chased them over the roof tops.

On another occasion, Cyril made a long rope ladder from clothes' lines and persuaded Ron to make a trial descent from his bedroom window. When they heard an adult approaching, Cyril withdrew the ladder in a hurry, which sent Ron hurtling down into a glass-covered scullery roof. Luckily, he was unhurt, but the glaziers were busy all next day.

Even Ron was horrified when Cyril took his role as a Zulu in his father's Sunday school play too literally and threw – to everyone's horror – his assegai across the school hall.

Just before both boys were dispatched to different schools – the parents made sure it was in opposite directions – they managed to have a ride on Doreen's, Cyril's sister's, motorbike, which they knew was out of bounds. Cyril roared out of Exmouth with Ron as passenger, but failed to notice that at one point of the forbidden journey, his friend left the pillion and was sent flying into the bushes by the roadside. Ron limped to the nearest house, where a kindly farmer's wife patched him up and Cyril found him, to his relief, unharmed. Ron then faced the indignity of beginning life at a new school in heavy bandages and wearing fingerless kid gloves, remaining knee- and knuckle-scarred for life.

In later years, Cyril became an outfitter himself and a local lifeboat enthusiast. In between, God relented and gave him some five years in the Royal Navy fighting in the Mediterranean, which incited the adult Ron to quip: 'No wonder Mussolini's fleet achieved little or nothing.'

Ron and Cyril went for a little more than two years to the same school, the Exmouth Secondary School, called 'The Grange'. Ron became a day scholar and began his chequered career on January, 17th 1924. His father's occupation was noted on the admission form as 'Printer and Stationer' and the family's address as Berlin House, Rolle Street, Exmouth. Ron left the Grange on April 1st, 1926, not only because of his various misdemeanours with Cyril, but mainly because of the 'Brickyard Scandal'.

His career at the co-ed Grammar School in Exmouth had distinguished itself not by academic brilliance, but rather by outrageous behaviour. Class friends, always marvelled at how any of Ron's rubbers seemed to gravitate towards the glue pot, which in those days was kept ready for use on a burner. Of course, this created an almighty stink. The woodwork master was not the only teacher, Ron drove round the bend. He held the school record for the highest number of misconduct marks and Saturday detentions in one term.

Both Mr. and Mrs. Delderfield, were more occupied with the running of their respective businesses than with the upbringing of their sons. They were frequently sent for by the headmaster of the Grange. This rather annoyed Ron's father, not so much on account of his son's misdeeds, but because he believed that it was the task of the schoolmaster to deal with pupils. Ron couldn't believe his luck, when his father thundered in one of those meetings in the headmaster's study: 'Sir, I am a busy man! I have received three of your facted notes beginning: I would like to see you re: your son this term. Don't send me any more. You get the facted salary for making him tow the line. I don't.'

Ron had a good reason for showing off: It was Doris. She was the daughter of a Wesleyan minister, and sat three seats away from him in class, displaying an incredibly demure expression. Ron did his very best to impress her – to no avail.

After a while, he lost interest and went out with René. René was Hazel's sister who was going out with Sandy, one of Ron's pals. In order to get rid of the sister on outings, Hazel pushed René in Ron's direction, who was rather taken aback when he was kissed for the first time in his life. Being a hopeless romantic, he felt committed for life and went through with a secretly held mock marriage ceremony in the park chapel. However, not much later, during rehearsals of the school nativity play, he became interested in Elsie, which led to his relationship with René ending in a blazing row.

In retrospect, he was convinced that this co-ed school had planted in him the seed that there was a living to be made from the study and practice of romanticism.

The only two school subject, he began to develop an interest in, were English and History. Owing to his father's newspaper, Ron occupied some sort of honorary position in the literary circles at the school. Some of his work was published in the school magazine *Exmothiensis*. This early success convinced him that he didn't need to study any other subjects if they had nothing to do with creative writing. Ron reported cheerfully about their Christmas party in 1925 in *Exmothiensis*, the magazine of Exmouth Secondary School:

'We had a jolly good time at the III.B and IV.B. party (to say nothing of ghosts on the lawn and hungry phantom faces pressed against the window panes) where they chose partners in a strange way, by each having the half of a proverb, e.g. 'A rolling stone gathers no moss' and then proceeded towards the dining hall, where we beheld the tables groaning under the weight of good fare, so we hastily relieved it of its burden, which we bore quite cheerfully. At the refreshment interval a Jazz Band came in, and during the next five minutes enjoyed itself thoroughly. We suspect that the enjoyment of the audience was not quite so great, but this may be wrong; the oranges may have been sour.'

The enjoyment and frolics at the Grange were to be halted abruptly, when twenty pupils were suspended after being found kissing passionately after school in the brickyard behind the playground. They were soon re-instated after it transpired that the scandalous behaviour had been started by a girl called Cis, who had a fatal fascination for the boys. She had passed the brickyard provocatively slowly for days, looking, as the boys believed, for romance. Finally, Ron's friend Ted Russell ambushed her, witnessed by a great number of pupils. The passionate kissing became rather a pastime for the Grange's students, but of course, the secret wasn't kept for long and the brickyards declared out of bounds for years.

This was the last straw for Ron's parents. They had never thought much of the mixed class system and decided that their son should join a private boarding school to make a gentleman of him.

SEVEN

The Unjust Sky and the Family
(1960 -1963)

'Don't you think you are overdoing it?' suggests May.

She is getting worried about Ron's frantic approach to churning out stories, his lack of exercise and his consumption of coffee and cigarettes.

'Don't answer that,' she laughs, perching on the far corner of his desk, not to disturb the mountains of papers.

'The last time you took a rest, you were bored stiff!'

She leaves with her slender fingers through the piles of critics for *Diana*. They are very gratifying.

The *New York Times* lies on top.

May reads: '*Diana* is a great love story... a charming novel recapturing with refreshing simplicity the awkwardness, excitement and delights of youth.'

May can identify with this; their courtship had been romantic, two years of long distance correspondence, snatched trips to London and endless cups of tea in Lyon's tearooms to keep warm.

The Scotsman wrote something similar: 'The freshness, sincerity and tenderly romantic mood of this novel will please Mr. Delderfield's admirers.'

May reads aloud the article *The New Statesman* has printed: 'I read this novel with steady pleasure. Constantly thoughtful of knowledge and fluently written, it rejects an uplifting ending at the last moment – for reasons befitting the mature approach of the whole.'

A little further down in the pile, May finds her favourite by John O'London: 'If this were the only novel that R.F. Delderfield had ever written, it alone would earn him the gratitude of generations of adult readers.'

'It was wonderful writing *Diana*,' Ron muses. 'All my romanticism responded to it, because so much loving intensity has gone into the writing of it.'

He smiles at his wife. 'It is one of those stories, you really do live as you read it – which is to say, of course that you fall in love with Diana and you suffer with Jan.' May knows that this novel has entirely captivated and possessed him.

'By the way,' May stacks the pile of newspapers and magazine neatly back onto the desk. She smiles enigmatically.

'Oh no,' groans Ron, 'don't tell me you want to move again.'

Since the early 1950s, they have moved no less than six times. May loves to design the interior of new houses and tends to fill them with antiques from auctions until there is no more space and they have to move to something bigger.

As a young couple, they had started from a house in Exmouth called 'Oak Park' in Bradham Lane and later moved to 'St. Cyr' in Douglas Avenue in Exmouth, before relocating to the Sidmouth area. Their first house there was 'Spion Cop' in Pebblecombe Regis on Peak Hill. By 1951 they were moving again to a most beautiful property called 'Knowle House'in Budleigh Salterton, which May turned slowly into a hobby farm.

'Do you remember the small holding?' They both burst out laughing.

They remember well how they quickly acquired an entire menagerie of animals. Their reasons for those purchases were rarely sound financial ones.

'I love the picture with Coalmine, Paul and Ron Hole.' May says. 'That horse was lovely and Christine, the cow, had such nice red hooves.'

'Did she really? I thought all cows have the same brownish coloured hooves.'

'No, they were definitely red, very pretty.'

'His memory must be playing tricks,' May smiles to herself.

'We were all a bit frightened of the geese except Paul,' Ron continues.

'Poor Veronica! Her pony was on the other side of the field from the geese's territory.'

'He looked so funny with the dustbin lid and a long broom rushing at them like a midget Ivanhoe,' recalls his father.

'The Valley of the Honking Death, we called their pen', May chuckles.

Luckily, they found Ron Hole whom they put in charge of the house, gardens, often the children and the growing menagerie of pets and farm animals. He was invaluable not least when the family moved house again and again.

May has also bought an ex-tollhouse on the A30 from Exeter to Torquay, where she tries to contribute to the family budget by buying and selling antiques.

Chris Woodhead from Honiton, an experienced antiques dealer himself and friend of the family, advises and supplies items for the shop. May is quite knowledgeable about antiques, but he suspects that neither May nor Ron have much business sense. They do not tell him that the shop is not as profitable as it could be, because Ron sells items at reduced prices to customers he likes. At the beginning of their marriage, May has attended a course on antiques and Ron thinks she has great flair. They love going to auctions, and he is enormously proud of his wife's ability to keep books and to make a profit..

The little toll-house also doubles up as a gallery for May's watercolour still-lives, which are decorative but not for sale. They are happy, she attending to customers, he writing in the back of the shop surrounded by three Napoleon figurines on his rickety writing table.

May is a compulsive visitor to auctions, and soon the toll-house becomes too small. They relocate to a bigger shop at Newton Poppleford. Ron moves his study to the first floor above the business and puts the finishing touches to *Diana*.

To Ron Hole's great surprise, he is suddenly given the order to organise two large furniture vans within the next forty-eight hours to go to Anglesey in the Menai Straits. When they arrive there, he can't believe his eyes: The Delderfields have bought a dilapidated house, which is smaller than anything the family has ever lived in and could certainly not accommodate the young couple as the handyman had hoped. Ron Hole decides to go into shared lodgings in the village and writes to his young wife that she is better off staying in Budleigh. He spends the first two weeks cutting back brambles to reclaim the wilderness that is supposed to be the garden. He thinks the only redeeming feature of the place is its spectacular view across the Menai Straits.

Not even a year passes, when he arrives in the morning and the house is empty. He finds a note written by May: 'My husband declared last night at twenty-to-eleven: 'May pack up, we're moving. I have woken Paul and we shall now drive through the night back to Devon. Please arrange the furniture van.' Luckily, Veronica is at boarding school at the time, so that they do not have to worry about her. She will follow later to their next address, 'Squabmore House' on Woodbury Common.

Why the family moves so often is anybody's guess. Ron Hole thinks it might have been in search of inspiration. May, who loves doing up houses, is also a driving force. Others are of the opinion that it has to do with the author's constant battle with the Inland Revenue. Ron has always railed that it costs him a fortune in taxes (£42,000 between the war and 1963) to stay in England, but he can not imagine living anywhere else, never mind write anywhere else. 'I might save money living in Switzerland, but the whole source of my inspiration is England; if I moved abroad I would die of artistic strangulation,' he confides in a reporter during an interview.

In the autumn and spring of 1962/63, only interrupted by a particularly harsh winter, Ron fulfils his dream of following into the footsteps of one of his favourite authors, J.B. Priestley, to travel the length and breadth of our island. This is much more to his taste than exposing himself to the rigours, inconvenience and dangers of journeys abroad. He travels for four months, visiting exactly the same places as his literary hero, three thousand miles from Devon via Somerset, Norfolk, Lincolnshire to York, West Riding, Sheffield and the Derbyshire Dales on his first leg.

The arctic winter that follows gives him time and space to write until April of the following year, after which he sets off again, travelling from Bristol to Chester, Western Lancashire, the Lakes, the Borders and the last town of England, Berwick; then on to Durham, Industrial Lancashire, Manchester and finally Warwick.

The account of these journeys is gathered in a small book titled *Under An English Sky*, which contains not only detailed reports of events and backgrounds, but also, in its introduction, the entire European history since the First World War and England's diverse roles during those years. He wants to bear this in mind while investigating what kind of England can be found now.

The result is an unfashionable reaffirmation of faith in England and the English, an unashamedly patriotic testament, ending with the optimistic conclusion that 'a people who had wrested basic rights from French kings, feudal bullies, bigoted Puritans, eighteenth-century landlords and Hanoverian martinets, were unlikely to surrender them to twentieth-century bureaucrats, who make it a habit of losing themselves in Whitehall pigeon holes where they were looking for precedents. Not at all events for long enough to matter. After all, for centuries now the English have lost the battles but won the wars.'

Two things have struck him as strange on his travels through

England: in all the pubs he has entered, nobody spoke about politics, as people do in other countries, and the second being the annoying inflexibility of shop opening hours. He dreamt more than once of late evening and Sunday shopping when he was low on provisions.

In spite of excellent reviews for the two *Diana* volumes, *There Was A Fair Maid Dwelling* and *The Unjust Skies*, the income from them cannot be compared to the revenues from theatre plays, radio and film adaptations and magazine articles. Writing romantic novels seems to be an indulgence, even more so than Ron's Napoleonic novels which attract a small but devoted and loyal readership.

Ron is not proud. He does not follow the aesthetic concept of the creative writer starving in an attic for his art. He has a family to provide for. Of course, he writes to entertain his readers, to amuse himself, but even more importantly, to make enough money to be able to afford to write in reasonable comfort and reasonably well-fed.

It is also important to him to be a good citizen. He gladly agrees to hold lectures at the Women's Institute, to lend his voice to the movement against horror films, to write articles in defence of the young generation, to take over the chairmanship of the Sidmouth Amateur Dramatic Society and to battle with Plymouth City Council to erect a plaque – which Ron is going to donate – on the Hoe foreshore to commemorate Napoleon's visit to the town aboard the Bellerophon in 1815.

He is furious when they turn him down, but experiences a great deal of Schadenfreude when in 1969, a French television crew arrives to interview him for a program on Napoleon's centenary to be broadcast that summer. Ron will proudly appear on French television, standing on Plymouth Hoe pointing to the Bellerophon's mooring on the Ham Oaze, hoping the Plymouth councillors will eat their heart out.

Ron leans back in his desk chair, resting his elbows on its wooden arms. He is pleased with *Diana*. He included many of his war-time memories into writing the second part, *The Unjust Skies*, which shaped Diana's role in the French Resistance. He often flicks through a little book called *These Clicks Made History*, which he edited while his war-time friend Stanley 'Glorious' Devon had provided the photographs to cover the fall of Le Havre. It was a far more illustrious end to Ron's military career than he could have ever hoped for. After all, its start had been rather less promising.

EIGHT

The War Years and *Worm's Eye View*
(1939 – 1945)

Ron Delderfield was a tall, big man, but he was neither athletic nor authoritarian. Furthermore, he was extremely short-sighted and not what one would call soldier material. However, he was very patriotic and felt compelled to report at the recruiting depot. It was not easy to get into anything except the Infantry, but he was finally accepted as a clerk. Considering his responsibilities for his father's *Exmouth Chronicle* newspaper, he could have easily avoided call-up, but then he had always had an enormous sense of fair play, and everything Mr. Hitler did in those months leading up to the Second World War, contravened that sense entirely.

After reporting at the recruiting office in April 1940, Ron went back home and waited, bored and anxious. In the third week of May, he was called to Uxbridge, where he was put in charge of half-a-dozen West Countrymen. This lasted exactly two weeks, after which everyone was sent home again. Ron returned to his journalistic duties for a further seven weeks and joined a slightly ridiculous group, called the Local Defence Volunteers, whose sole duty it was to patrol the cliffs to scan the horizon for enemy invasion. As another concession to the war effort, Ron sold his Austin Seven and acquired a bicycle to drive around the district.

It was a relief, when his call-up papers arrived and he was told to report to Cardington within the week. May decided to move back to her family, so they let the house in Exmouth, installed Punch, their terrier bitch, with the family who owned the local pub before Ron took May up to Manchester. They spent their last afternoon together going to the pictures to see *Gone with the Wind*, after which Ron took the train to Cardington. He only stayed there for seven days, where he shared a bell-tent with nine other volunteer reservists. He was immediately asked to write for a column called 'My most exciting moments'.

Between June 1940 and August 1942, Ron was sent to Morecambe, twice to Blackpool, twice to Buckinghamshire and twice to Staffordshire. May came to visit him for two weeks in Morecambe, but they were not allowed to share a billet; she therefore rented a room, where they spent their free time together.

In August 1940, Ron was sent to a huge camp in the Midlands to do 'General Duties' in administration. In reality, the work consisted of wading through endless piles of paper and answering incessant telephone calls. He became rather depressed, in spite of a very understanding Sergeant by the name of Bill Williams.

To counteract his boredom, Sergeant Williams referred Ron to the bomb disposal squad, but they only took him along once, because he had been more of a hindrance than of real assistance. Instead, he was asked to write the Christmas pantomime. They gave him three days and the corporal's billet, from which he appeared breathlessly but satisfied with the play *Binbad the Airman*. It was an excellent production under Ken Annakin, the nephew of the late Lord Snowden (Chancellor of the Exchequer in the first Labour Government) who, after the war, would become very successful in the theatre world. The scenery was borrowed from the Birmingham Repertory Theatre and his dame was a very popular W.O.Discip, called Tich Reick.

Christmas 1940 was a strange affair. It was extremely cold in May's rented bed-sit with only a single bed and a Christmas meal consisting of two mutton chops. But they appreciated that they could be together at all and that Ron was posted in a small town only eight miles away.

Meanwhile, a little drama had developed in Exmouth because the pub owners moved away and could not look after Punch any longer. May and Ron were upset and unsure what to do with the poor dog, but then Evie Birks, the famous Madame Butterfly of the Carl Rosa Opera Company and her sister Hilda stepped into the breach and took charge of him. The Delderfields had acquired another two friends for life.

Ron wrote nothing more in the following months, but made some important theatrical contacts. One of them was Basil Thomas, a light-comedy writer who was associated with the Salberg Repertory Theatre, The Grand at Wolverhampton.

Between May 1940 and November 1943, Ron was posted in thirteen different camps, among them Cardington, Morecambe and Cosford, where he was duty clerk and in the autumn, upgraded to Leading Aircraftman. At the beginning of 1941, he was sent to Bridgnorth where he learnt that he had been promoted to the rank of corporal, and in the late summer of that year, he ended up in Blackpool, where May joined him and got herself a job at the local newspaper.

The next posting was the Personal Dispatch Centre at West Kirby in the Wirral, then Moreton-in-the-Marsh, Hinton-in-the-Hedges, Peplow, Renscombe Down on the Dorset coast, back to Cosford, then Cranwell – the Sandhurst of the RAF – and Stannington in Northumberland.

Towards the end of the summer in 1941, Ron filled in papers for a commission, but they were returned with the remark: 'Insufficiently educated to be an officer'. He did not like to admit it, but it piqued him a little. Furthermore, he was worried that he might be posted overseas.

Ron's general duties bored him enormously, but however unsettling the constant changes of camps were and however boring the endless paperwork was, at least he felt safer than he would have been at the front of war action.

In the bed next to him slept Wyndham Samuel from Worthing who sensed that it was an anxious time for Ron. Every morning he would smoke furiously before going down to the Orderly Room to check whether his request for cancellation of the overseas posting had come through. All had been issued with tropical kits, but none of them knew their ultimate destination. The unavoidable rumours on the grape wine made things only worse.

In the evenings, they used to have a fair amount of banter and discussions at the hut – they were not allowed out for security reasons. Ron, in a subtle way, would make a simple comment which would start an argument. His RAF friends would recognise some of the topics in his later writing.

Two days before they were all dispatched from West Kirby to embark on the 'Stratheden' at Gourock on the Clyde, Ron came back from the Orderly Room with the lines of worries gone and his face wreathed in smiles. His overseas posting had been cancelled. Everyone else ended up in Alberta, Canada.

Meanwhile, May's job at the local newspaper helped to keep financial worries at bay, but she had to give it up and return to Devon because she expected her third baby. After two still-births, she was not going to leave anything to chance.

Ron was dispatched to several more airfields. His most favourite of them all was Hinton-in-the-Hedges. There he made life-long friends and had the time of his life. They called Hinton-in-the-Hedges a 'Hide and Seek' camp because for the greater part of their posting, they seemed to have been forgotten by the RAF and were left to their own devices, not that they grumbled! It took weeks before one of them, Joe Lane, discovered that they had a runway!

Robert Russell was sent to Hinton-in-the-Hedges in early 1943. After having made the rounds of the orderly Room, Station Sick Quarters and Stores, he reported to a WAAF seated next to a large desk bearing a sign that said DELDERFIELD R.F. – CORPORAL, DUTY NCO ADMIN. After having been fed in the Cookhouse, Robert reported to the NAAFI – Navy Army & Air Force Institute or, as rechristened by Ron 'Never Ave Any Fags In'. He came upon a group, enthusiastically drinking half-pints of some excruciatingly awful-looking beer and being shrouded by a thick Woodbine cloud. They were discussing corporal punishment and its unacceptability. As 'Delder' warmed to his theme, his eyes beamed with passion, whilst the others listened enthralled and with admiration. When Robert joined in the conversation, Ron's eyes lit up and he suddenly remembered that they had met as long ago as 1941 in Wolverhampton. Robert had been a senior student there at the Technical College. The College's amateur dramatic society sometimes helped out the Grand Theatre, where the well-loved Basil Thomas was in charge.

'You were the one, Basil Thomas introduced to me and my wife at the Grand in Wolverhampton,' Ron exclaimed.

Robert had been bowled over when this exuberant man had extended a hand to him and had immediately launched into a vivid description of the town, his living away from the unit – which at that time was the RAF Station at Bridgnorth – and discussed with him local wartime drama entertainment. May, tall, attractive with high cheek bones and a wide smile and auburn hair, remained on the edge of the conversation, occasionally slowing her husband down or correcting some of his statements. They gave out an air of immense togetherness and closeness, with an underlying feeling of sorrow. Ron had spoken of a three-act-play, he had written together with Basil Thomas, titled *The Matron* which he had now re-named to *This Is My Life*. The production of this play, Robert had assumed, must have prompted the Delderfield's visit. Shortly afterwards they left because Ron had to catch the 'railway stampede' in the morning back to his RAF station.

Now they met again. As Robert settled into a routine of duties at Hinton-in-the-Hedges, he joined the ranks of the many who were attracted to 'Delder' like magnets. They would envy him his heaps of mail, which he willingly shared with them. Nevertheless, he would groan at the ultra-sympathetic words of his agent, then Margery Vosper (the sister of an early British film star, Frank Vosper) had written to him, if another play had been refused or another tax demand had been received.

'You lucky old sod, Delder!' Robert would say to him and Delder would snarl back theatrically: 'Tax, tax, am I not taxed sufficiently on my very life style in this Air Force, this durance vile?'

Ron always made his wife May laugh because he could account for every penny he spent and felt guilty meeting his comrades at the Three Tuns Inn for a pint. However, on pay-day, having cycled to Kings Sutton village, he would buy ale for all his colleagues. The following morning, he would send the rest of his pay addressed to Mrs. May Delderfield in Exmouth.

When lack of funds denied the airmen the hospitality of the local pubs, they were most welcome at the Memorial Hall in Charlton Village. No-one appreciated this more than the chronically hard-up Delder. The ladies supplied them with coffee, tea, spam sandwiches and Sweet Corporal cigarettes. Ron would hold court and fascinate everyone including Lady Birkenhead, who kindly introduced Ron to another member of her family, Lady Eleanor Smith, an established authoress. His invites to liquid lunches and much literary advice at Lady Eleanor's home was cause for much leg-pulling by his mates left behind in the Memorial Hall.

His time in the RAF had a surprise in store for Ron. He had been brought up to believe that women thrown together would be getting on each other's nerves quickly, but he found that the sex solidarity in the WAAFeries put the men, who were frequently bickering, to shame. High-spirited as the girls were, they loved Ron's ebullient nature. He gave many of them nicknames: There was the 'Firm Buttocked Kay', the 'Deep Bossomed Joan' and the 'Dimple Kneed Dora', all three delectable ladies of excellent virtue. 'Deep-Bossomed' Joan was in charge of massaging Ron's and Robert's sore temples whenever they appeared in the morning with a hangover after a night of heated discussions and war-time ale. Reg Frampton of Exmouth 'would have liked to have a pound for every pint we drank.'

In order to indicate the end of the temple massages, Joan used to plant a lip-sticked kiss on Ron's then already balding head, the traces of which he refused to wipe off all day. This earned her the second nickname 'Hotpot', while her friend Judy, who was rather prim and did not approve of Ron and Joan having a joke, ended up being called 'The Fridge'. However, both girls stepped willingly into the breach, when Ron wanted to retire to a backroom and concentrate on doing some serious writing.

And write he did, mainly for the little theatre he was trying to establish from a second mess hall. This was encouraged by his Squadron Leader Sweetlove, whose wife was keen to play leading parts in Delder's productions. Rehearsals took place in the Sweetlove household and the amateur actors were well supplied with sausages and mash. Everyone was helping out to put *To Salute The Soldier* week variety show on stage, which was a series of sketches and pantomimes. Then followed a comedy *Scattered Seeds* about a houseful of refugees of different nationalities, and an adaptation of *Printer's Devil*, a play Ron had written before the war. Joan played Miss Strindal, Joe Lane was one of the devils, Derrick Robinson was the stage electrician, 'dimple-kneed' Dora played the piano before the show and between the acts. The Squadron Leader Sweetlove and his wife had roles and Ron's good friend Robert Russell played the sub-editor Nathaniel Hurst.

It was all enormous fun, more so than wading through the endless stream of paperwork in the Central Registry. They called themselves the 'Hinton-in-the-Hedgehogs Concert Party', of which L. Smale was in charge as the W.O. Admin and Entertainment Officer. Ron cajoled, persuaded, flattered and, in the name of RAF morale, invited the officers to take part in their productions. Of course, there was no stage, just a large, virtually unused empty Second Airmen's Mess, but there was abundant talent, into which Ron tapped enthusiastically.

First the group astonished the local draper by buying up enormous quantities of blackout material in cotton and some rather lovely lilac cambric, which was to be made into stage curtains by the sewing machine operators, usually sewing fabric for the repair of aircraft fuselages. For days, 'Delder' and his pals, surrounded by airmen in working overalls, sawed, chiselled and hammered away to erect a stage. Then the rehearsals began in earnest. Delder took the part of the senior owner of the seaside newspaper press and Robert played his son Nathaniel opposite him. The play involved practically all airfield personnel; no one was safe once Delder got going! One of the actors realised with horror that his long-awaited leave coincided with the dates of the performance, but he was persuaded to cut short his leave and return to camp three days earlier. After the show had finished, he was given another pass to return to his home in Great Yarmouth with an extra five days leave as compensation.

'Yes, he does bully and cajole dictatorially,' they agreed, 'but he extracts every ounce of loyalty from those air force men and women committed to his play – and yes, we all love it!'

The whole camp turned up for the two performances and half of Hinton-in-the-Hedges as well.

They were a spirited and close-knit group of people, thrown together by the war. Corporal Barker, who played 'Bumble' in the *Printer's Devil* production, invited the entire cast to his wedding in North London. They steered the bridegroom with precision from pub to pub, after which the throng of quite intoxicated airmen, led by 'Delder', assisted him on his way to the altar, and from church to the reception, where celebrations continued.

Ron Delderfield had organised the day-to-day running of RAF life efficiently. The cooks at Hinton appeared to depart on twenty-four hour passes more than one would normally have expected, thanks to the administrations in the Orderly Room Central Registry, of which Ron was in charge. In return, all the occupants were awoken at 6.30 a.m. in the morning by Cook No.1. He ran into the billet carrying a huge aluminium-handled jug, containing about a gallon of boiling hot tea, two large tins of Libbys milk and a mug of sugar. At seven o'clock, Cook No.2 would appear with a newspaper parcel of hot fried bacon sandwiches, which 'Delder' distributed to his cronies.

In military matters, 'Delder' did not do quite so well. A couple of times, he managed to lose contact with his squadron in the fog, but nobody could remain exasperated with him for long, particularly as he laughed with them at his mishaps.

To everyone's chagrin, Ron was transferred to Peplow in November 1943 as a registry clerk. There he met a high-spirited LACW called Anne MacEllroy. When she realised that he was a playwright, she provided him with endless titbits of information from the WAAFery, which earned her a dedication in one of his later books: 'For Anne of Peplow; Vivandiere and Cheerleader, 1943 – 1970.' Anne would remain a dear friend, visiting May and Ron regularly in Devon long after the war. However, it was not an altogether happy time at Peplow.

Ron was still suffering from the repercussions of a dressing down at Moreton-in-the Marsh. He had hardly arrived, when he had got into trouble after a high-spirited night out on the town. He had only followed 'the call of nature' in the bushes on the way home, nothing more than that, but obviously a grave offence in the eyes of the authorities. Ron's feeling of humiliation lasted a long time and May registered with great amusement that her husband would go to great lengths to avoid that town from then on.

Anxiety of being posted overseas, frustration with the limitations of a desk job and loneliness because May was so far away, contributed to ill-health. When Ron developed shingles, May rang frantically from Exmouth to make sure he was well looked after. Only Robert Russell's reference to her advanced pregnancy and the need to avoid stressful journeys prevented her from rushing to Ron's bedside.

He had hardly recovered when he heard on the radio, that the great Max Reinhard, the famous impresario, who had promised to produce his passion play *Spark in Judea*, had died. And then the worst blow of all hit him: May's third baby was stillborn, too. As in the two previous pregnancies, she had developed a kidney infection. The death of the babies was also blamed on Ron being rhesus negative. The young couple were heartbroken. Ron rushed to her side trying to console his inconsolable wife, but after a couple of weeks, he had to return to the RAF camp.

Many brief, reassuring visits to May followed whenever possible, and on one of the journeys home, on a crowded bus returning him to camp, he had an inspiration for a play. He wrote the synopsis there and then on the bus in thirty minutes and called it *Worm's Eye View*. He took another nine months to perfect the script about a landlady, who exploited her resident RAF lodgers mercilessly.

Ron read out the well-worn script to most of his colleagues and did not always get the reaction he expected. His friend Joe Lane thought, that he had never heard such crap in all his life; as a 'worm' living this life, he failed to see the humour. Ron would agree with him years later when he was overheard muttering: 'If I had written *Worm's Eye View* after the war, thinking back to the many unhappy lodgings I have endured, it would not have been a comedy at all.'

The story was an accumulation of ideas and experiences from spring 1940 to winter 1943, a small revenge on the type of landladies who depended on the income from renting out rooms to soldiers, but who resented their presence and treated their lodgers with disdain and meanness.

Apart from that, he wanted to capture the sense of oneness with the millions of unknown men, the sense of kinship that made them support each other in a time few relished. No amount of post-war disillusionment could tarnish Ron's admiration, love and respect for the ordinary British man and woman ever again.

'Delder' had continued his battle to become an officer and had filled in numerous 1024s, but, to his annoyance, he was considered insufficiently educated. By 1943/44 it had become a point of honour to sustain the contest. Thirty-three months after having left as a newly passed-out recruit, Ron returned to the Officer Cadet Training Unit in Cosford as a corporal. On Christmas Eve, he and his fellow trainees were sent on leave as temporary pilot officers. In the new year, Ron was dispatched for two months to Cosford and then on to Stannington in Northumberland, where he took an Admin. course. His room mate there, Abrams, submitted 'Delder's name to the Public Relations branch, following which Ron was interviewed by Wing-Commander Lord Willoughby de Broke, the Deputy Director of PR at Air Ministry in London.

By the end of February, Ron Delderfield joined the staff of Wing-Commander Dudley Marker, a well-known Fleet Street journalist. He was sent straight away to the feature department, known as the P.R.3, which housed a collection of the most wonderful literary men in uniform. There he met John Pudney, the novelist and poet; Vernon Noble of the *Manchester Guardian*; F.W. Wallbank, a Yorkshire schoolmaster, who wrote after the war essays on the English scene; the novelist and short-story writer H.E. Bates; Eric Partridge, the lexicographer and etymologist; Hilary St George Saunders, the author of *The Green Beret*, the story of the Royal Marine Commandos. This was a change of scene indeed!

Ron stayed in lodgings at No.17 Clarendon Road, Holland Park where he had the first floor front room. Sometimes, he took refuge from the bombs in the lighthouse-type home of his friend, the actor Walter Hudd, or with Ken Annakin at Norbiton. On Sunday, the 18th June, he was nearly killed by a doodlebug while on duty at the Royal Military Chapel at Wellington Barracks.

Ron Delderfield was soon sent on missions to the Sussex coast and to Biggin Hill airfield, but one of his greatest war time adventures was still to come. In early September 1944, he and the photographer

Stanley 'Glorious' Devon were sent to France for six days to cover the fall of Le Havre and to report about fifty-six bombed centres in France and Belgium.

They flew over to Bayeux in a Dakota, but had then to hitchhike most of the way. It was not too unpleasant, as the British were held in great esteem by the French. They travelled on to Caen, Rouen, Bolbec and Yvetot, before being flown home on an ancient Harrow aircraft. Ron wrote the text to Stanley's pictures which were published under the title *These Clicks Made History*.

Ron was dispatched for a second time to the Continent in October 1944. This time he was accompanied by a P.R. photographer, a cine-cameraman and a driver for the van. The senior photographer was Bernard Bridge of the *Blackpool Gazette*. They based themselves at Brussels from where they visited at first Louvain and Courtrai.

They spent Christmas in Toulouse, where Delder sold his boots to provide for a meagre meal to mark the day. They then worked their way northwards to Bergerac and Limoges. All in all, they travelled seven thousand miles across Europe until mid-January.

By then, Ron had forgotten all about his play *Worm's Eye View* which he had written on a bus and handed over to his friend Basil Thomas. Ron was most astonished when he collected forty-eight fan letters from the American Express Office in Paris, informing him of rapturous reactions to the play's performance at Wolverhampton the previous autumn. The resounding success of *Worm's Eye View* at the Wolverhampton Grand did not come a moment too soon. Ron had sometimes been rather downcast about the lack of interest in his work in civvy street, and it became more and more difficult to appreciate the advice of his old friend, the actor Walter Hudd (or 'Dickie' as he was known): 'It is futile to resort to depression over your writing; never ever give up!'

In October 1944, Ron's luck had changed and *Worm's Eye View* had run for one sensational week at the Grand Theatre in Wolverhampton.

Corporals Robert Russell and Ken Kenyon, one of 'Delder's' most trusted friends, were requested to represent the author, who was somewhere on the Continent, at the opening night on Monday, the 30th October. After they had obtained permission from their Wing-Commander, they travelled excitedly to Wolverhampton where Basil Thomas received them cordially, introduced them to the cast and ushered them to their front stall centre seats. The play was ecstatically received by a packed house; everyone seemed to have a relative in the RAF and, recognising the characters in the play, the laughter was loud and long.

Ron's agent had also sold the touring rights to a Midland manufacturer by the name of H.J. Barlow, who took it in April 1945 to Norwich, Westcliff, Preston, Bolton, then during victory week to Cambridge and finally to Hammersmith in London, where the critics were not all that flattering.

Ron remained grateful to his friend Basil Thomas for the rest of his life. 'He was a businessman and the only theatre man who has never found it necessary to tell white lies,' he wrote later. Ron appreciated Basil's honest criticism and encouragement and was sure that without him, there would never have been a *Worm's Eye View*.

Ron Delderfield spent VE Day, May 18th, 1945, trooping with thousands to Whitehall. He was hoping to see some 'mafficking', so he walked from Trafalgar Square to Piccadilly Circus and Buckingham Palace. After waiting expectantly for a while, he realised that the Royal Family would not come out onto the balcony. Baffled, he went up to Charing Cross Road, from where he took a tube back to his lodgings in Holland Park. He complained to the landlady that he had seen 'very little mafficking' and concluded regretfully 'that the English are useless at mafficking and how it got into our language, I'll never know!'

A few days later, curiosity took him to Fort Road in Bermondsey, where he had spent his first childhood years. It had been bombed and rosebay willow herb was sprouting from the pile of rubble that remained.

He was glad when, on the 4th November, he was finally demobbed and free to return to his wife May, their adopted daughter Veronica, who was by then eighteen months old, and his beloved West Country.

The *Exmouth Chronicle* building opened in 1939 on Chapel Hill, Exmouth.

West Buckland School, North Devon

A ticket for an early dramatic venture.

THE CORPORAL'S ASTONISHING PLAY

A BRILLIANT RE-ENACTMENT OF AIRMEN'S LIVES IN THEIR LANCASHIRE BILLETS DURING THE WAR HAS CREATED AN ALL-TIME BRITISH DRAMA RECORD. THE PLAY, WHICH RECENTLY PASSED ITS TWO THOUSANDTH PERFORMANCE IN THE WEST END OF LONDON, WAS WRITTEN BY A FORMER CORPORAL AND HAS NETTED HIM THOUSANDS OF POUNDS.

T HE NIGHT OF DECEMBER 19, 1945, was particularly unpleasant: wild gales lashed the east coast, while in the condemned cell

counter " at Release Depots for ex-airmen prepared to tip the staff suitably.

No other musical or non-musical play has achieved such a run. "Blithe Spirit" 1,997 performances; "Me and My Girl" 1,646: "Arsenic and Old Lace" 1,337.

Headline of an article in *REVEIW* and theatre programmes of *Worm's Eye View*.

The programme for *The Queen Came By* and a page from *PLAYGOER* which covered the production generously.

Opposite: An account of the Delderfield's attempt at farming.

Ready for the chase.

Mr. Hole with RFD's son Paul.

Theatre programmes for *All Over Town*
with the review in *THEATRE WORLD*.

For an author who flees from his success

LADIES AND GENTLE-
MEN, I give you a new
Champion of England: Ron-
nie Delderfield, author of
that record-breaking farce
"Worm's Eye View."

He lives in E n g l a n d,
though it costs him a fortune
in taxes—£42,000 since the
war.

New champion

He scarcely ever travels
out of England—when the
Russian Minister of Culture
invited him to Moscow to
spend his rouble royalties,
Delderfield stayed here.

May, his wife, told him:
"You with your big mouth.
In fifteen minutes you'd be
inside Lublanka jail." So he
didn't go.

By Arthur Pottersman

and intellectual stimula-
tion.

"I could go to live in
Switzerland but the whole
source of my inspiration is
England.

"I would lose touch with

Madness of Mr. Sermon,
out on July 22.

Before Sean Connery became James Bond
played a gipsy airman in "On the Fiddle." H
he talks to the author, Ronnie Delderfield, a
Eleanor Summerfield.

A cutting from *THE DAILY SKETCH*, July 1963 showing Ron Delderfield with
Eleanor Summerfield and Sean Connery discussing *On The Fiddle*,
Sean Connery's first film..

R.F.DELDERFIELD

back from his tour of the United States,
considers that 'special relationship'...

RFD was a regular contributer to magazines
such as *THIS ENGLAND, DEVON LIFE* and
COUNTRY LIFE.

RFD wrote several historical books about
Napoloeon and his exploits and based stories in
the same period.

A selection of Ron's prodigious creativity, with some translated into several languages.

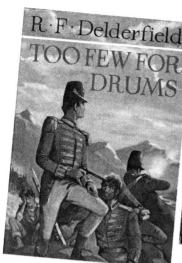

R·F·Delderfield
TOO FEW FOR DRUMS

R.F. Delderfield
Too Few for Drums

Bestselling author of To Serve Them All My Days

SEVEN MEN OF GASCONY
R.F. DELDERFIELD

F. DELDERFIELD
The Adventures of Ben Gunn

AUTHOR OF A HORSEMAN RIDING BY
R.E DELDERFIELD
GOD IS AN ENGLISHMAN

R.F. Delderfield
GIVE US THIS DAY

PÄIVIEN KULTAINEN KETJU

R.F.Delderfield

KARISTO

R.F. DELDERFIELD

Elämää Sorrelin laaksossa

R.F. DELDERFIELD

Elämää Sorrelin laaksossa V

KARISTO

R F Delderfield

NINE

Spring Madness, a *Horseman Riding By* and Napoleon
(1963 – 1967)

The Delderfields live now at Peak Cottage, a mad-cap residence high upon a cliff near Sidmouth. Ron won't allow for the hedges to be cut. 'If I could enjoy the stunning views from my study window, I would never write a word,' he defends the state of the garden.His estate agent, Peter Eley (who later on owns an antiques' shop in Sidmouth called 'Delderfields') can't stop shaking his head about this man who buys houses nobody else in their right mind would buy.

Ron has just finished his latest novel *The Spring Madness of Mr. Sermon*, which will be published on the 22nd June by Hodder & Stoughton. It is the story of a hitherto reliable schoolmaster and husband, who suddenly breaks out and heads for open country, freedom and happiness. Mr. Sermon sheds the accumulated responsibilities and trappings of a lifetime and sets out with only a few rough clothes and two books of verse. Ahead lies Mr. Snugg, an odd little man who teaches him the antiques trade, the generous-hearted Olga and Rachel, the fascinating young girl with whom he discovers romance again.

Ron has written *The Spring Madness of Mr. Sermon* with enormous underlying sympathy, understanding and wit, supporting the notion that 'it is never too late to be what you might have been.' It is not only about the menopausal folly and panic of a forty-nine year old man; it is about the possibility of leaving an unsatisfactory life and proverbial rut; it is about the idea that every day could be a new beginning if one only drummed up enough courage. It is also an assurance that romance is not only for the young and beautiful, but for people of all ages and in everyday situations, particularly the middle-aged who sometimes missed it in youth; it is also about finding out about yourself and discovering hitherto unknown talents, strengths and longings.

The American publication of *Mr. Sermon*, a modern day Mr. Chips, earns acclaim as 'satisfying as the readers of R.F. Delderfield have come to expect… Filled with real scenes, real people and real action, the characters are so beautifully drawn, the settings are so exquisitely worded, and there is such a basis of common sense under the whole plot that this book is delightful reading.' (*Best Sellers*).

Ron's literary output remains enormous, but nothing has brought him nationwide acclaim so far. In parallel to the romantic novels, Ron has never ceased to write historical novels fuelled by his passionate interest in the Napoleonic era.

'Lockart's *The Life of Napoleon* started me off. I found it in Mr. Appleby's second- hand bookshop in Exmouth,' Ron remembers.

'When was that?' asks May

'Just after I went to work at my father's newspaper, I suppose... Vic Whitworth and I used to go to Mr. Appleby's.'

'Oh, Vic your school friend from the Grange?'

'Yes. He got hooked as well. They were marvellous books. Carlyle's *French Revolution* was written like an eye-witness account of the chaotic and terrible happenings in France between 1789 and 1795. It was fascinating!'

Young Ron's collection of books about this historical epoch occupied soon three shelves in his private library, and was the source for many stories about Napoleon. He started with a series of disconnected episodes called *The Adventures of Cornet Cavendish* and Maron de Marbot became a kind of patron saint.

In 1949, he wrote in *Seven Men of Gascony* (published by Werner Laurie Ltd., London) about the sharpshooters in the 87th Regiment in Napoleon's Grand Army, from the height of its glory to the crushing climax at Waterloo. The description of these seven soldiers was treading the typical Delderfield furrow: showing a warm regard for human beings against the fascinating background of their careers, leading from Lobau to captivity in England, escape, Moscow, Leipzig and Waterloo.

Next Ron worked on a story called *Farewell the Tranquil Mind,* while still living in a house aptly named 'St.Cyr' in Douglas Avenue in Exmouth. It told the story of an East Devon family, the Treloars, who lived dangerously, mixing farming with smuggling in the 1700s. David Treloar, the sole survivor after calamity struck his father and brothers when they perished in a smuggling raid, has to flee to France. There he becomes witness to the French Revolution, living in Paris with the family of an old wigmaker. In love with his patron's daughter, David soon realises that the hope for more humanity is fading and that the revolutionary movement has got out of control and become a bloodthirsty monster. Ironically, David Treloar ends up in 1794 in an English prison suspected of being a spy. This book was also published by Werner Laurie Ltd. in 1950.

Ron's strength lay in a deep appreciation of history, which did not debar him from presenting his characters as men and women, who, a hundred years ago, lived, loved and died, much as people do today. The warm regard for people's trials and struggles shines through and the story is a mixture of local folklore, hearsay and historical facts written with brilliance and imagination.

'Veronica and Paul were responsible for *The Adventures of Ben Gunn*,' Ron recalls.

'They pestered you every time you had finished reading *Treasure Island* to them,' May smiles.

They wanted to know what happened to their favourite character, Ben Gunn, after the story had finished. Ron felt compelled to write a sequel. He offered it to publisher Michael Sadleir of Constable's, but it was refused. It gave Hodder & Stoughton a chance to take over, beginning a long and happy business relationship with the author.

Life Magazine was full of praise for what had started as a story written for Ron's children: 'R.F. Delderfield is building an imposing artistic social history, that promises to join those of his great forebears in the long, noble line of the English novel.'

A Scottish critic made Ron very proud by calling him 'A blood-and-thunder brother of Robert Louis Stevenson.'

By 1963, Ron has written two more Napoleonic novels: *Napoleon in Love* and *The March of The Twenty-Six*.

Napoleon in Love began its life as a novel, but was turned into a play for the Pitlochry Festival in 1960. It was a sequel to *The Mayerling Affair* and lasted two hours. The size of the cast was at first a problem which was satisfactorily solved by the ever optimistic heart of the Pitlochry Festival, Mr. Kenneth Ireland, who proved excessively tolerant. It was not a conventionally-shaped drama, but a chronicle play presented in a series of scenes, closing with dramatic black-outs.

It begins with the announcement of Napoleon's divorce at Fontainebleau from Josephine, who could not present him with a legitimate heir. Napoleon's conscience is more ravaged than people imagine when he meets eighteen-year old Marie Louise of Habsburg, whose training for marriage is incomplete to say the least. The story describes the groom's matchless experience with women, the Imperial wooing, the birth of the King of Rome and the return of Napoleon from the debacle of 1812.

The dialogue incorporates many of the sayings by or about Napoleon which history has transmitted, and it shows the tenderness he was capable of as a lover.

The *Pitlochry Sunday* proclaimed that 'Mr. Delderfield can be trusted with history' and that out of the three plays reviewed that year, it was 'the one in which the company, despite the large casting demands upon it, easily showed up best'.

The March of The Twenty-Six followed shortly afterward. It is the story of Napoleon's marshals, recounting their very different backgrounds and their rise to power, their loves, intrigues and quarrels and their reaction to the end of Napoleon's days of triumph. Ron was clearly at home with this subject and concluded that in waging war, Napoleon was less guilty than his opponents and that almost every war he engaged in was forced upon him when he was simply striving to reform France in peace.

Now, in 1964, Ron has two important matters to organise: The publication of *Two Few For Drums*, another Napoleonic novel, and Veronica's betrothal to Lieutenant Burton Richard Edward Persse, the great-nephew of the famous Alty Persse, racehorse owner and trainer. The groom has recently returned from active service as a Royal Marine in Aden and Tanganyika and has since his return played cricket for the Royal Marines, the Royal Navy and occasionally, Sidmouth Cricket Club.

In a letter to his publisher, Robin Denniston of Hodder & Stoughton (now Hodder Headline), Ron tries to combine Veronica's betrothal to his illustrious son-in-law-to-be and the publication of his most recent book, *Too Few For Drums*, which is about the peninsular campaigns of the Napoleonic era.

The book's unlikely hero is Ensign Keith Graham of the 51st Foot, who is cut off from the main British army during the withdrawal to the coast after the victory of Busaco. He finds himself taking charge of a motley band of a sergeant and seven private soldiers and a Welsh camp follower called Gwyneth. They stick together through many desperate adventures to a tense climax, in which the nineteen-year-old becomes a true hero.

Ron is very proud of this book and thinks it is the best technical piece of work he has ever done.

'It has the lightness of construction, a kind of suspense, that belongs to a thriller and it seems to me to read very smoothly, giving an accurate picture of the times and the characters of Wellington's scum of the earth,' he writes to his publishers.

In the same letter (dated 12th February, 1964 – Ron's 52nd birthday), he explains: 'What I would like to emphasise is the reaction to the anti-hero cult of the last ten years in novels – which has been brought into sharp focus, I feel, by the enormous fill-up to national morale supplied by our army's fire-brigade actions in Cyprus and East Africa... For these men were the very first of Britain's 'Tommies', later to win such distinction in two world wars.'

Veronica's wedding takes place – undisturbed by publishing frenzy – at the Sidmouth Parish Church in the presence of both families. The reception is held at Peak Cottage followed by a honeymoon in Italy.

Ron, himself a charming, hopeless romantic, is not averse to the occasional platonic flirtation.

His particular fondness of his favourite WAAF, Anne of Peplow (later Mrs. Honeyman of London), was well known, and so is his pleasant working relationship with Jane Eustace of the Promotions Department at Hodder & Stoughton, whom he addressed as 'My Dear Indefatigable Jane!' More than once he praises her work on his behalf in glowing terms and is astonished at her efficiency: 'I am sure Pitman's page was all your doing. What a wow of a publicity girl you are. I expect you can cook as well!' (11th August 1963).

On another occasion he writes: 'I would adore writing long letters to you, but how would they look in Hodder's files and what material they might yield a biographer!!'

In another letter he enthuses: 'My Dear Jane, perhaps you 'got' some of this yesterday or perhaps I was incoherent because I am so unaccustomed to unloading myself to a 'business executive' who walked off the train looking like the cover of a glossy magazine! It was such fun meeting you and I feel sure you will be able to do something with this material.'

However, Ron and May's marriage is solid as a rock. They are dedicated to each other and it is very unlikely that May will ever have a serious contender. As his publishing friend at Hodder, Eric

McKenzie puts it: 'Ron might spend an evening being pleasant and flirtatious and taking the girl home, but it all ends outside her bedroom door.'

On January 3rd, 1965 Ron indicates to his publisher, Robin Denniston: 'I am punch drunk on that book', referring to his most recent, non-historical novel, *A Horseman Riding By*. He adds with hardly veiled desperation: 'I hope to God something comes of this book. I can't last out much longer and have already made enquiries about returning to journalism and seeking a regular job somewhere.'

It is not so much the quality of his writing that worries publishers, but the length his sagas seem to grow into.

Walter Minton of G.P. Putnam's Sons, New York, is rather alarmed and sends a hurried letter to their British counterpart saying: 'I rather rue the day I urged him to go forth and write a big, broad canvas novel for the American market. It seems to me that Ronnie has confused his dimensions; his depth is linear – through the generations rather than across the canvas. There is nothing wrong with the novel, but I am a little bit dubious about our ability to sell a novel of that length.'

In the end, his eventual American publishers, Simon and Schuster, relent and take the plunge, printing all 1,151 pages of *A Horseman Riding By*, which sets a precedent for future novels.

Writing it and its sequel, *The Green Gauntlet*, Ron discovers a good deal about himself. He falls hopelessly in love with its main female character, Claire Derwent, because she has something that combines all the physical and spiritual assets he most admires in women: She is pretty, buxom, possesses any amount of common sense, is impulsive, generous, loves the Valley she lives in, and shares her husband's hatred of cities; she is also gloriously uninhibited, while remaining feminine.

Ron never ceases to acknowledge his debt to Devon, which was not his native county but which he has learnt to love passionately. He has a talent for observing as the outsider, while feeling only as a native son can feel. Devon has become the canvas on which he paints his pictures.

Ron describes *A Horseman Riding By* as 'a sort of rural *War and Peace*,' while the critics call it 'a Galsworthian chronicle of a Devon valley, its squire and inhabitants.'

Craddock has settled there, after being invalided out of the army and the Boer War. He first falls in love with the unpredictable Grace Lovell, who champions the cause of the suffragettes. She never really shares her husband's simple dreams of belonging to the Valley and caring for the Estate tenants. Instead, she chooses persecution and rare, short-lived triumphs in pursuit of her own ideals. She even schemes for her own replacement at her husband's side. She knows Claire Derwent is a woman of the Valley, who has loved Paul from the moment she has met him, and who turns out to be the perfect match.

The underlying theme of *A Horseman Riding By* is Paul Craddock's feeling of responsibility for the tenants and craftsmen of the Shallowford Estate in the West Country Sorrel Valley. In a way, it is an antidote to the blatant materialism of the sixties.

At first, Ron thought, he might call the novel a *Portrait of a Patriot*, but, as he explains in an interview with Alan Greenhalgh, 'the Americans understand a 'patriot' as being a chap in a cocked hat on horseback like Paul Revere.'

To find a title for the first volume of his most recent novel, Ron instigates a little competition at his old school at West Buckland, where one boy comes up with *A Horseman Riding By.*

The idea of the second volume, *The Green Gauntlet*, is prompted by the shape of the imaginary valley: 'This Valley, from a thousand feet, looks like a gauntlet, a great, finger-spread glove, made of green and rust-coloured leather. It's all wrinkled and seamed, and the two predominant colours are unevenly spaced, blotches of both appearing here and there but without any plan.'

By April 1965, Ron is deeply involved in the sequel, *The Green Gauntlet*, which is finally published in May 1967. It takes the Craddock's family history into the Second World War with intentions to follow it 'into the stale fifties, the Profumo sixties and perhaps a slant on the Common Market situation'. It is the principle that wins out. Paul Craddock wins back parts of the Valley which had been snatched by developers; his ebullient twin sons replace their silly set of values of money-making and being trendy by discovering what is really important in life, the kind of belonging that their father has always known. Simon, the son from his marriage with the rebellious Grace Lovell, who at first has displayed his inheritance of defiance among the rebels in Spain, finds his niche in life as a gifted school teacher; Whiz, the posh daughter, never changes and gives them lots of reasons for sniggers and laughter until she eventually mellows; Mary never leaves the Valley and marries Rumble Patrick, while her brother John chooses a career in television, in which he can publicise his father's cause, the conservation of Valley life. Paul Craddock himself remains an unrepentant chauvinist and manages to hold his own against his exasperating brood, because his arguments are genially expressed and his memory is diabolically accurate.

After the publication of both books East Devon becomes Delderfield country.

The order of precedence, as in all of Ron's work, is background – theme – character – plot, 'the plot being the cumbersome wheelbarrow on which the other three are wheeled before the public.'

In an article in *Devon Life* (March 1965) he remembers: 'Looking back I find it odd to discover how insistently Devon tugs at creative impulse, how mercilessly she jogs the elbow and sometimes drives a man hopelessly off course', as happened as far back as *The Avenue* saga, which was firmly rooted in Addiscombe/Surrey, until one of the main characters found herself suddenly swept to the pine and bracken country of East Devon.

'Why quarrel with your bread and butter that happens, by chance, to be your jam as well?' the author jokes. Walks through the coppices on the eastern border of Muttersmoor, west of Sidmouth, never fail to inspire him.

It takes Ron nearly four years to write both volumes of *A Horseman Riding By*, during which the characters become so real to him that deaths shock him.

'By the time I have got to the end,' he writes cheerfully to a friend, 'I shall probably be dead. But it will be worth it. The British are the most civilised people on earth and are nearer to being perfect than any other race. That's what the novels are about.'

As in all his novels, Ron draws from his own past. The canvasses of great sweeps of woods, the walls of rhododendron, heather and gorse of the West Country, the river Whin and the town Whinmouth, obviously standing for Exe and Exeter, make a constant appearance, and so does London, the Kent/Surrey border and the arduous Exmoor cross-country run, for which the young West Buckland boarder had shown some aptitude, and which is still believed to be the toughest public school run in the entire country.

While Ron is immersed in the creation of *The Green Gauntlet*, the family change their address once more – this time they move only thirty yards from Peak Cottage to the Gazebo, a circular-shaped thatched house perched on the edge of the cliff, on the spot where Queen Victoria's father caught his death of cold in 1819. It was like a Martello Tower with a thirty mile sea vista.

On the brink of fame and success as a novelist, Ron bombards his publisher with letters, suggesting strategies to promote his books in the media, on radio and television, via the School Inspectorate (to which his old friend 'Romeo' Boyer belongs) and even offers to write a book of modern history from 1914 to 1964 for children of the ages of twelve to fifteen for the school service.

He needn't have worried – the critics take him to their hearts and even such illustrious people as Peter Cushing, Bonham-Carter and Jeremy Thorpe count themselves among his admirers.

The *Times Educational Supplement* has this to say: 'The writer is an accomplished storyteller and handles his many characters with skill. He can describe the solemn magnitude of such scenes as the funeral of Sir Winston Churchill, and yet he has a countryman's keen eye for such tiny objects as the marking of a peacock butterfly.'

The *Sunday Times* enthuses: 'his compassionate portrayal of the life-cycle produces an ache some way below the mere intellect for a dying way of peace.'

The opinions of local newspapers, *The Express & Echo* and *The Western Morning News* are equally important to the author and he gleefully describes their positive reviews in a letter in June (1965) to his London publishers, Hodder & Stoughton.

The BBC contributes to the wave of promotion by discussing *The Horseman Riding By* on radio programmes such as THE BOOK AND BOOKMAN TALK on the Light programme, followed by WOMAN'S HOUR, AN AUTHOR VERSUS LIBRARIAN discussion and a promise to have some of Ron's previous books read on air.

A first inkling, that all was not well with Ron's health, was conveyed in a defiant letter to Tam at Hodder & Stoughton as far back as 1962 titled 'My New Year's Resolution: 'To enjoy tobacco as I did before they told me every puff is another coffin nail.'

But on October 30th 1965, Ron has to inform Robin Denniston that 'I go into hospital for an op. on Nov. 9th for 10 days. After that I have cancelled all engagements away from here for the month.'

After the operation, on December 8th he writes again, referring to the previous month as 'the desperately involved period I have been living through', and that he 'was happy having had the chance of talking 'shop' with Robin during his brief visit to the Delderfield home'.

Hodder & Stoughton send a prompt reply wishing him a speedy recovery. The letter also speaks of anticipation of success of *A Horseman Riding By* 'for all of us' and the hope that Ron might fill the gap left by the recently deceased author, Howard Spring, who had been tremendously popular with the library readership. Lastly, they express their regret that Ron would not be able to join their Christmas party.

Thoughts of Christmas are not uppermost in Ron's mind. In fact, he finds that festive time of year rather trying.[5] In an article in 1962 he expresses these feelings: 'My thoughts, hopes and prayers for Xmas are simple and reactionary. When I hear carollers piping about Wenceslas 'poor man' coming in sight carrying winter fuel, I shall congratulate myself that it is not as yet rocket fuel. What we all need between this Xmas and next Xmas, I feel, is a Space Pause, a period to digest some small portion of the scientific knowledge and power we have won during the last two decades, before our happy-go-lucky Eggheads do something really final to this tortured planet. Briefly, let us bend our efforts on both sides of the Berlin Wall to put common sense, kindness and toleration into orbit.'

By November 1963, he has not changed his mind and pens, when asked to write a Christmas feature for Stanley Jackson: 'I long since came to terms with Christmas and my patron saint of the foul festival is Scrooge, a prophet if ever there was one! I now lock myself in my study from first light and work, re-emerging with some 20,000 words on Boxing Night, buttressed by the smug satisfaction that my digestion is unimpaired, and I have the means of paying some of the bills incurred by the Conspirators who are at pains to pick my pockets and break my creative rhythm every December! These are my Christmas plans for 1963.'

After his operation, Ron immerses himself once more in the Napoleonic era and writes *The Retreat From Moscow* which is

---

5. This does not mean that he did not participate in the family Christmases. His daughter believes that these comments don't ring true and insists that they always had a fantastic time at Christmas. He was too fond of the family that he would behave so badly. The author can only speculate that his bout of illness had put him in the mood to have a good moan about the state of the world.

dedicated to the Officers, N.C.O.s and men of the Grand Army of the year 1812. It is the story of Napoleon's campaign into deepest Russia, the emperor's biggest mistake, and traces the whole affair from its over-confident start to its disastrous end. For the Allies, it meant the turning point of the war against him, because he had shown himself to be capable of this colossal blunder.

Again, Ron takes great care to introduce the reader not only to the historical events and military details, but to the triumphs and failings of illustrious and common soldiers alike.

The book is published in 1967, lavishly illustrated with plates of Alexander I (Emperor of Russia), Napoleon, Marshals Ney, Oudinot and Murat, Eugene de Beauharnais, the Grand Army crossing the Niemen and maps of deployment, battles and routes taken.

Now that Ron is fully recovered, most of 1967 is taken up with another novel called *Cheap Day Return*, a detailed analysis of first love and a tempestuous, inappropriate attraction that ends in disaster for its main character, Kent Stuart, a small-time photographer in Reddiffe Bay. After thirty years in exile from his home town, he returns and re-lives the haunting events of his first passion, which resulted in a shameful scandal and a collision crash of the main characters.

It is a simple story and full of heart-warming conclusions, human beings can draw when tested by fate. When Stuart Kent asks the man, whom he has hurt most, what happiness is, he answers: 'All but the freaks, people like my wife, want the same thing…To be needed in one way or another by a small group of people, badly needed by one or two, moderately so by a dozen others. That's the most important requirement and that's what most of us spend our lives trying to achieve in one way or another. Everything else is substitute'.

But by then it is too late and the young lover has lost his youth, his happiness and the girl he had wanted to marry.

Ron also picks up again the same theme used in *The Green Gauntlet*, the trend to modernise familiar places; the way Paul Craddock had to watch in horror as the bulldozers moved close to the boundaries of the Shallowford estate to replace its fields and woods by airports and caravan sites, so Kent Stuart finds everything unrecognisable on his return.

There is a gentle knock on Ron's study door. It opens to a small gap and a brown, tousle-haired head and a happily smiling face peeps round the corner. May's slender body is still hidden by the door and the slim fingers of her left hand hold the door ajar, indicating that she will go away if she is disturbing

'Come in, I have just finished.' His heart always lifts when he sees his wife and he smiles at her.

'Another letter from Dora.' May, now fully in the room waves a piece of paper.

Ron always looks forward to news from his old friends and never fails to respond to them in spite of churning out one novel after another.

'Oh, I see, she has moved,' he comments while reading the letter. 'I know Addington. It's fairly close to Addiscombe, where I used to live just after the First World War.'

A few days later, in September 1967, Dora Haken, 'quite the prettiest WAAF from Hinton-in-the-Hedges' receives a detailed progress report: 'Your new address brings back memories of my first primroses in 1918. The woods on the left of Spout Hill and the country between Shirley Road and Cudham were a wilderness of farms, lanes and coppices!'

Dora has also mentioned a book she found with his name, but only similar initials. Ron explains in his reply that his brother Eric writes guidebooks and that 'the similarity in initials is a damned nuisance.'

Ron ends the letter with a promise to look her up when next in Croydon and to inscribe a book for her as a memento of 'that crazy camp'.

There is also some family news to report: 'Veronica lives with her helicopter pilot husband (in the RM) in Singapore and has one son called Simon. Her brother Paul is on a farriers' course at Hereford.' Dora is particularly delighted with the photograph Ron encloses of him and his Labrador 'up on the original of "Shallowford" plate'. She can't help laughing when she reads on the back: 'Haven't I gone bald!' As far as she can remember, he has always been like that.

'I hardly write theatre plays anymore,' Ron mentions in his letter to Dora. 'The sagas and biographical novels of Napoleon take up too much time.'

His new readership hardly remembers that he had started his writing career as a cub reporter on his father's newspaper, writing theatre plays in his spare time.

TEN

Theatre Plays, Radio and Films
(1928 – 1956)

After leaving West Buckland School, Ron attended a commercial college in Exeter. He still lived with his parents and spent a good deal of his time travelling from Exmouth to Exeter. On his journeys, he read poetry, which soon bored him. He thought he might try Shakespeare; however, in the various volumes of *Famous Plays of The Year* by a firm named Gollancz, he discovered much more easy-to-read playwrights and came to the conclusion that it must be a piece of cake to write plays.

As it happened, it took nearly twenty years before one of Ron Delderfield's plays would be successful and, based on this success, others written years earlier, would be accepted for performance in one theatre or another.

His very first attempt at writing and staging a play was at boarding school and ended nearly in disaster. The play was called *Murder in the Pulpit*, appropriately written out of boredom during Sunday church services. When it was performed by the school, the author's instructions were taken quite literally, so that the actors had to be pulled apart before someone was killed.

From the age of eighteen, Ron spent most of his free time writing plays, sent them off including a stamped addressed envelope for an eagerly awaited reply.

One of his attempts was inspired by a set of cigarette cards called *Famous Escapes*. The play carried the title *One More Bed*; its subject was the escape of Napoleonic prisoners from Pembroke jail with the added complication that the one, under whose bed they dug the tunnel, was a traitor.

As Ron had not taken any advice from books on how to write plays, but set about it 'like an amateur carpenter goes about making a rabbit hutch', it turned out to be rather heavy to digest due to many passionate and lengthy monologues.

In the pursuit of finding a producer for *One More Bed*, Ron met Edgar Middleton, the playwright, who had written *Potiphar's Wife*.

This chance encounter led to more encouragement and one of the best pieces of professional advice anyone had ever given to the young aspiring writer: 'Write what you damn well please; don't try and write for the public. If you do, you won't please them and you won't please yourself. Write what you want to write and you've got a million to one chance of pleasing them by accident!' Ron took this very much to heart.

Another supporter at Exmouth was Percy Barrow, whom Ron met three times a week over two years for an hour to improve his style and under whose tutelage he practised and wrote a long school story entitled *We Third Formers*.

Ron's first comedy, entitled *The Windfall*, the story of a Camberwell family who had won a prize at the Irish Sweepstake, was read by the actor Walter Hudd while he was on holiday in Exmouth. He gave him the second most important piece of advice: 'Write about what you are and what you are in. Use your work as a reporter to observe everything with the eyes of a writer, making mental notes of even the most unimportant-looking news item, and consider everyone you come in contact with worthy of at least one good story. It will sharpen your memory and develop your skill of mental photography!'

Ron's other passion, the cinema, inspired him to write the next play *Pebble in the Pond*, the story of a group of people meeting in a railway waiting room. The 'talkies' cinemas had arrived in Exmouth in the winter of 1929/30, and Ron was fascinated.

His friend and mentor, the actor Walter Hudd bought a six-month option for thirty pounds on Ron's next play, called *Fleet Street in Lilliput*, to prove his belief in Ron. Many years later, it would be performed and become well known as *Printer's Devil*.

Meanwhile, Ron had fallen in love and had married the lovely and ever supportive May from Manchester. However, it was a blessing that Ron had the job at his father's newspaper, which paid the bills for the young couple, while he continued to write plays in his spare time. May contributed to the family finances by buying and selling antiques and taking in lodgers.

In 1937, the young producer of New Plays, Bill Heaven, took an interest in putting *Spark in Judea*, a religious play, on the stage of the Ambassador Theatre in the West End. It was indeed performed on a Sunday night. Ron held his breath until the critics came out:
They found the play 'interesting' and 'promising', which did not give much away. It turned out to be only a flicker of success, snuffed out almost immediately.

Around the same time, Ron, wanting to show the manuscript of his play *Twilight Call* to an actor of a touring company realised that his only copy had been sent to the Birmingham Repertory Theatre two years earlier. As it had never been heard of since, he asked for it back and was most astonished to receive a telegram by return saying: ' Don't ask for it back now, we are doing it next week'.

Mistrusting his good fortunes, Ron travelled immediately to Birmingham and found his name on a hoarding. It was immensely flattering.

The day after the opening night, at least one critic, Maurice Wiggin from the *Birmingham Post*, was encouraging by titling his article: 'More please, Mr. Delderfield'. Ron took May up to Birmingham in the following week to see the play. She was naturally very proud of her husband.

After a fortnight, the play sank back into oblivion. They had reached the end of another cul-de-sac. In a way, Ron was not too unhappy, because he had not entirely enjoyed the company of actors, whom he found volatile and argumentative.

Ron had been writing plays for ten years now, all in all fifteen, of which four had been actually staged. The production, he had been most proud of, was *Printer's Devil* in late July 1939, produced by Andre van Gyseghem and with an enormously good cast including Walter Hudd, Curigwen Lewis, Eliot Makeham, Charles Bascomb, Charles Hawtrey, Arthur Young and John Garside.

The public reaction was inconclusive and only drew obscure comments like the one James Agate wrote: 'Good enough to fail instantly in the West End!' Ron had no idea what to make of it.

Again Ron did not relish the experience working with theatre folk. There were terrible tensions behind stage, and he was constantly asked to re-write scenes, pandering to the ideas of various actors, the producer and the director. It baffled him why theatre people chose a script to perform and then wanted it changed radically into something the author had not intended it to be.

After a week at the Q Theatre, the play was transferred to the Embassy Theatre in Swiss Cottage, where it drew surprisingly excellent reviews. This was followed by performances in Northampton and at the Civic Repertory Theatre in Bradford. Ron also had an offer of eight hundred pounds for the film rights of *Printer's Devil*. Finally, his career as a playwright seemed take off, only to be thwarted by history and fate putting a spoke into its wheels: The Hitler-Stalin Pact was signed in August, and on September 3rd all theatres closed.

The RAF made good use of Ron's writing talent during the war years by asking him on various occasions to write and produce variety shows for the entertainment of the troops. He also carried on working on his own projects, sheltered in back rooms by sympathetic WAAFs, so that he would not be disturbed. The enthusiastic Hinton Hedgehogs Concert Party helped to perform a new comedy called *Scattered Seeds* about a houseful of refugees of different nationalities, and an adaptation of *Printer's Devil*.

Ron had been given hope that his Passion play *Spark in Judea* would be produced by Max Reinhard, only to hear a few weeks later on the radio that the famous impresario had died.

Nothing seemed to go right for him until one day he scribbled on a bus, which took him back to camp, the synopsis of *Worm's Eye View*, the story of the horrible landlady who made the lives of her soldier lodgers a misery.

The resounding success of *Worm's Eye View* in the week of 30th October 1944 at the Wolverhampton Grand Theatre under Basil Thomas did not come a moment too soon. Ron had been sometimes rather downcast at the lack of interest in his plays in civvy street.

Some members of the original cast of *Worm's Eye View* were to achieve nationwide acclaim: Gwen Berryman became Mrs. Archer on the radio and Iris Russell turned into a renowned West End actress.

Basil Thomas had also a hand in the second run of *All Over The Town*, which was basically a re-write of *Printer's Devil*. The Wulfrunian audience received it ecstatically and the press confirmed that Ron Delderfield was a successful playwright.

The Darlington Telegraph wrote: 'R.F. Delderfield's play has the great merit that its author is describing a corner of life of which he has intimate knowledge and is transcribing it vividly to the stage. Consequently, his story of journalism in a small seaside town has excitement and tension. We are held from the beginning to end by the story of Nat Hurst's fight to turn *The Sandcombe and District Post* from a sleepy and sycophantic rag into a live newspaper. Mr. Delderfield has considerable knowledge of local politics and a quick eye for local politicians. His play is a good honest piece of work. Walter Hudd plays Nat with the honesty the part demands.

It could hardly be better done. Curigwen Lewis plays his fiancée with tact and charm, and there is good work by Arthur Young, Eliot Makeham, William Hellbroun and half a dozen others.'

By now, *Worm's Eye View* had been taken on tour, ending up in London to erratic reviews. Ron's play about Florence Nightingale, *The Spinster of South Street*, which had been performed in 1944 at the York Festival and been taken on tour with Baliol Holloway and Jean Forbes-Robertson, was performed around the same time as *Worm's Eye View* at Hammersmith and drew equally unflattering remarks.

Before Ron had decided to take the plunge to put *Worm's Eye View* on a West End stage, he had asked his friends of the Exmouth Players to perform it for the Exmothians. It was received with great enthusiasm and 'the whole of Exmouth fell about laughing'. His old friends Queenie Greenaway, Kay Gibbens, Raymond Moxey and Mr. and Mrs. Sleeman remembered sixty years later, what fun it had been and how honoured everyone in Exmouth had felt that Ron should choose to try out the play, that promised to be a great national success, in their town, and how thrilled they had been by the audience's favourable reaction and the great hilarity it created. They knew from Ron personally, that that dreadful landlady, Mrs. Bounty, had indeed existed, and that whenever the play was performed at Morecambe, the whole population turned out to have a jolly good laugh at the expense of the woman everyone recognised.

Anthony Bazell (who played the role of 'Duke', the Don Juan in the play) had been pestering Tony Hawtry of the Embassy Theatre while on tour. When he ran into the elated Ron Delderfield on demob day, accompanied by an equally overjoyed H.E. Bates, he gave him the good news.

However, Ron returned to Devon – to his wife May, little Veronica, whom they had adopted, and his job at the Exmouth Chronicle, thinking that *Worm's Eye View* would go the way most of his work had gone so far, a skirmish and then lying still.

In the long run-up to the first night in the West End, Ron had met up with Ronnie Shiner for lunches,who was supposed to play the lead in *Worm's Eye View*. He was immensely grateful to the actor who never lost faith. The play finally opened on December 4th 1945 at the Embassy Theatre.

No-one was more surprised than Ron, when it went ahead and the reviews were ecstatic.

Beverley Nichols at the *Sunday Chronicle* wrote: 'This play made my ribs ache ... yet we laughed. And I would like that sort of laughter to ring through Britain, from class to class, wiping away all bitterness'.

The *Sunday Express* printed: 'Frank, honest and lowbrow. I hope it runs and runs.'

Mr. Darlington of *The Telegraph* enthused: 'Full of good comedy and might prove very popular.'

And Nora Alexander at *The Mail* wrote: 'Managers are heard but seldom seen! ... The next time a manager starts that line 'My Dear Girl, find me a new play', I shall go straight out and buy him a ticket to Exmouth.'

After two weeks, *Worm's Eye View* was transferred to the Whitehall Theatre in London, which at first was a financial worry, but soon the play built up a reputation by word of mouth, so that by spring it netted around £2,000 per week. When the lease ran out, the play was taken on tour for nine weeks, after which it returned to the Whitehall, and did run and run, breaking the London record for straight plays. The previous record had been held by *Chu-Chin-Chow*, but *Worm's Eye View* broke the all-time British performance record with 2,243 performances, a run of five years and seven months until June 1951 – exactly as his clairvoyant landlady during the war, Miss Colyer, in London's Holland Park, had predicted! The success of the play was consolidated when it was made into a film in 1950.

When asked to explain the secret of the play's success, Ron mused: 'The comedy arises out of ordinary situations, readily recognisable by any man or woman who has served in the ranks. These are the people – and there are millions of them – who have paid to see *Worm's Eye View*. They like to laugh at themselves, and the piece now has a certain nostalgic appeal.'

It certainly captured the spirit of comradeship which had developed between men from all walks of life.

Ron was proud of having captured this spirit. Just after the very first success at Wolverhampton, his old friend Robert Russell had asked him for permission to produce and present the play with an RAF cast of serving airmen and women throughout Bomber Command. 'Even the C.O. thinks it is a great idea', he wrote enthusiastically. The author sent back a simple reply: 'It belongs to you blokes!'

The action of *Worm's Eye View* is set in a Lancashire boarding house, where five widely contrasted airmen are billeted. The house is dominated by a grim landlady and her son Sidney, who both hold the airmen in contempt. They try to dominated, that is as far as one can dominate such characters as Porter (played by Basil Lord), the one-time barrow-boy, who arrives with a case of black-market goods; little Taffy (played by Eric Davies) to whom everything happens; Pop, the wise, kindly godfather (played by Jack Hobbs); the self-styled Casanova known as 'The Duke', (played by Anthony Bazell); and the wavy-haired decent fellow, Mark (played by John Valey). The theme of the story, which runs through the scenes of slapstick comedy (bare feet in jelly, tea upset over Taffy's face, raids on the pantry) concerns Mark's love for Bella, the landlady's step-daughter. Eventually the downtrodden husband, Mr. Bounty learns to revolt and bolt for freedom. The 'Duke' goes for aircrew training and Mark leaves to become an officer.

Immediately following its original London run and having gone on tour, *Worm's Eye View* came to the White Rock Pavillion in Hastings with most of the original cast. The staff at the local jeweller's shop were ex-RAF men and members of the local RAFA branch; of course, they had all gone to see the play. To their delight, one morning, the actress Janet Barrow, who played the fierce landlady, came into their shop to have her wristwatch adjusted. When they told her how much they had enjoyed her performance, she pointed to the inscription on the back of the watch case; it said: To Janet on your 1,000th performance W.E.V. – with thanks R.F.D. Laughingly she confirmed that her character was based on a real person in Morecambe and that said woman was as unpopular as ever.

The additional income was very welcome to the Delderfield purse. Indeed, for the first time, the family did not need to worry and could spend money on a second-hand Ford. A little later they stretched to a second-hand Daimler from the showrooms of Mr. and Mrs. Boobyer in Exmouth. Ron and May gave parties for their old Exmothian friends and introduced them to the theatre community whenever someone visited from London. The Delderfields were enormously generous hosts, and even some of the more pompous artists, who sometimes caused May to nod off in the middle of the general jollity, were warmly welcomed.

Secretly, Ron found it difficult to feel at ease with theatre people. He could not see them as real people; they were so different from the ones he had known all his life. They lived from hand to mouth, their gaiety was as brittle as their promises and peppered with frequent bouts of melancholy. Ron felt that their friendships did not go very deep and were not as reliable as he expected friendships to be.

Ron found it also quite ruinous to travel so often to London to oversee productions. He preferred to stay in the West Country, keeping in close contact with his Exmothian friends. He also kept in correspondence.with many comrades from the war years.

Worm's Eye View had not only made Ron Delderfield a household name in the theatre world, but opened stage doors for some of the numerous plays, he had written over the years.

Peace Comes To Peckham was produced on October 2nd, 1946 at the Embassy Theatre in London and subsequently at the Princes Theatre, WC1 with Leslie Dwyer as George Palfrey, Chloe Gibson as Nurse Ironside, Peter Scott as 'Erbie Gilpin', John Wyan, Jeanetter Deeley, Valentine Dunn, Ursula Howells, Lionel Blair and Jefferson Searles. The producers were Anthony Hawtry and Wallace Douglas. *Peace Comes to Peckham* is a three-act comedy about the upheavals and the impact of American soldiers on an English family when they begin courting their hosts' daughters and turn them into GI brides.

By June 1947, Ron had re-written *All Over The Town*, known previously as *Printer's Devil*. It opened on June16th at the Wolverhampton Repertory Company, again under the tutelage of Ron's old friends Basil Thomas and Derek Salberg. In the cast were Helen Sessions, Peter Vaughan, Hugh Falkus, Anthony Sagar, Leslie Yeo, June Moir, Gerald Cluff, Con Kenna, Sally Newland, Gwen Berryman, John Laurence, Dorothea Rundle, Bob Anderson, Joan Rogers and Jack Betherington. The play transferred to the Playhouse Theatre in London on October 21st, 1947 under the direction of Terence De Marney and with a star-studded cast including Peter Neil, Rosalyn Boulter, Richard Carr, Gordon Phillditt, Peter Scott, Alec Finter, Arthur Seaton and Sydney Monckton.

The reaction of the audience was considerably more positive than some of the reviews, like the one by the *Theatre World*, who 'could not draw a profound or moving conclusion from the editorial policies of the *Sandcombe Clarion*, but after all, there is some freshness in seeing a small community reflected in terms of the local paper valiantly fighting for its soul.'

This was exactly what the author intended with his writing: the important social message that made people think. In an interview with Peter Drake of the *Western Morning News* in August 1047, Ron was quoted as saying: 'I feel strongly that it is possible to establish an important social theme within the framework of laughter. James Agate agreed: 'There is more humanity in his pair of braces than in all of the highbrow plays of the last thirty years.'

By the end of the 1940s, Ron was drawn between writing books on the Napoleonic period, on which he was a recognised authority, and plays or light comedies which represented the main source of his income.

The period between 1948 and 1955 saw the birth of many more Delderfield plays; some were staged in theatres, others were produced in film versions.

The Bride Wore An Opal Ring had been inspired by the questionnaire, Ron had used while he was working as a local reporter for his father's newspaper. This questionnaire was sent to the happy families about one week prior to the wedding, in order to avoid omissions or errors when mentioning guests, gifts and outfitters in the *Chronicle*'s write-up of the following week. The play was produced for television and shown in 1948.

All Over The Town was made into a film by Ian Dalrymple and Derek Twist, with distinguished actors such as Sarah Churchill, Cyril Cusack, James Hayter, Bryan Forbes and Stanley Baker in the cast.

The Queen Came By was performed at the Embassy Theatre and later at the Duke of York's starring Jean St. Clair and Thora Hird. It is the story of an ageing and ailing milliner in a Brixton emporium in the year of Queen Victoria's Diamond Jubilee. The milliner harbours an unaccountably maternal affection for a young orphan apprentice fresh from a convent. The girl is seduced by a man of bad character, confesses to the older woman and disappears. The milliner brings the girl back and persuades a young man to forsake London and his prospects in business, art and politics, and to take the girl instead to the wilds of Cheshire to work on the land to keep her.

The character portrayals and period atmosphere found acclaim, but the story was considered too far-fetched. This did not stop the play to go on tour over many years. It was still performed from 25th June to 10th July 1083 at the Connaught Theatre in Worthing.

In 1950, Ron wrote *Sailors Beware*, which he described as an Elizabethan Improbability in one act. It launched the career of the actress Peggy Mount.

1951 saw the completion of *A Wagonload of Monkeys*, a sequel to *Worm's Eye View* which was performed at the Savoy.

Where There Is A Will was played at the same time at the Garrick and was turned into a film in 1953.

Worm's Eye View had been put on the big screen two years earlier under the direction of Jack Raymond, the producer Henry Halstead, starring Ronald Shiner as in the theatre play, Garry Marsh, John Blythe, Bruce Seaton, Digby Wolfe, Everley Gregg, Diana Dors, Eric Davis, Christina Forrest, William Percy and Jonathan Field. Ronald Shiner had always believed that *Worm's Eye View* would be a big success and had never lost faith in the play.

In 1952, Ron's mother died after a long illness, and his father married almost immediately an old friend of the family, a very quiet lady, who understood and appreciated Delderfield senior's irrepressible temperament. It suited Ron and his brother Eric fine that their father continued to be so independent-minded. Ron didn't miss his mother much as he had never been particularly close to her.

Before moving with his family to the large Shortwood House in Budleigh Salterton in 1954, Ron churned out furiously one play after the other. It had become a financial necessity, since he had decided to give up the editorship of the *Exmouth Chronicle*.

The one-act comedy *The Old Lady Of Cheadle*, who according to the author's note did exist in the shape of a Mrs. Skyring of Cheadle, never rose above the amateur dramatic society level. It was about a woman who had loyally supported the Royal House with parts of her income during the entire exile of the Stuarts and was thrilled to witness the return of Charles II.

Golden Rain was to be more successful. After having been staged at first by the Windsor Repertory Company and then on three nights by the ever-enthusiastic West of England Theatre Company in Exmouth, it was screened on television in July 1953 with Brian Worth and Rona Anderson in the roles of Roger and Catherine Strawbridge. Roger, a country clergyman in a parish called Tidingforde-Stukeley, was battling with problems presented by his parishioners and his pretty young wife. She had secretly used a half-share pools win to improve their grim situation in respect of their finances and accommodation. The vicar found this method unorthodox, if not unethical, for a clergy household.

Glad Tidings was another of Delderfield's plays that was released as a film. Walter Rilla was solely in charge of the screenplay and direction, and the cast consisted of Raymond Huntley, Barbara Kelly, Ronald Howard, Jean Lodge, Terence Alexander, Diana Calderwood, Laurence Payne, Arthur Howard, Brian Smith, Harry Green, Roger Maxwell, Yvette Wyatt and Doris Yorke.

In December 1953 the Q Theatre put on a production of the re-named *Where there is a Will*, now *Follow the Plough*, in which a cockney inherits a West Country farm and decides to become a countryman to the horror of his sisters, with whom he shares his inheritance.

The Orchard Walls, a story of first love between two adolescents and the reaction of school staff and families was shown at the St. Martin's Theatre with the actors Valerie White in the role as headmistress and Gillian Lind, Helen Horsey, John Charlesworth and Cyril Raymond in the other roles. Everyone remarked that the author came down very much on the side of the young couple in this play.

In spite of both plays – *Follow the Plough* and *The Orchard Walls* – being considered by the critics rather dull, laborious and overloaded by characters and subplots, and nowhere near as funny as *Worm's Eye View*, the public seemed to enjoy them, so that *Follow the Plough* was even transferred in June 1954 to the Garrick.

Peace Comes to Peckham was the Saturday play on the Home Service in March, *Spark In Judea* became the easter Sunday television play and *Golden Rain*, the story of the vicar's wife who won the football pools, was adapted for television by Nigel Kneale, produced by Leonard Brett and televised on July 31st, which pleased Ron enormously, because he personally thought that *Golden Rain* was his best play to date.

Ron remained prolific, writing twelve plays in the following two years, of which the better known ones were *The Guinea Pigs*, a one-act comedy for women only, which had entirely to do with the WI; then there was *The Rounderlay Tradition*, another all women comedy; this was followed by *Glad Tidings*, which was performed at the Grand Theatre in Croydon, directed by Keith Beattie and performed by the Croydon Repertory Players; *This Happy Brood* was the story of a business magnate suffering a nervous breakdown, while his three spoilt children plan the distribution of his wealth, scuppered by a mother with her own agenda.

Where There Is A Will went on tour in February and March, travelling from Nottingham down to Exeter with a new cast, featuring in the lead role the radio and television star Eric Barker, supported by Bill Owen as the crafty Cockney, and Billie Whitelaw and Edward Woodward sustaining the love interest.

In spite of all this hectic activity, none of these later plays achieved the success of *Worm's Eye View*. They were published by Samuel French, Kenyon Deane and Felix de Wolfe & R.S. Stone. Many more did not make it into print

By 1955, Ron had enough of being a playwright, often commuting to London, Croydon or wherever performances took place. 'My heart was not on the stage,' he used to say later. 'The trouble with a lot of modern work is that too often the strident style obscures an interesting message. People wanted plays about sex and violence which are only part of life. To me the real hero is the ordinary chap, the middle-aged bank clerk saving up to pay his way, to educate his family and to keep his head above water.'

Ron did write another play, a historical one for the Scottish Festival called *The Mayerling Affair*, but he felt that 'they were just as mad as everyone else in the profession. The 'cat-nap' of Napoleon, wrapped in his cloak on the incarpeted floor of the Tuileries, snapped the long, snarled cord which had bound the author to the theatre.

Television and radio left him equally disillusioned: he did not get a bean for TV repeats and on one occasion, when they expected him to alter the conclusion of a script, so that Josephine, Napoleon's wife, would turn out to be an English spy, relations with the BBC became rather strained.

A last recording in February 1955 featured Thora Hird as Emmie Slee in *The Queen Came By*. The film world used two of his scripts,

Where There Is A Will and *The Orchard Walls*, which was released as *Now And Forever*, adapted by Michael Pertwee in cooperation with Ron. This was followed by the adaptation of Derrick Boothroyd's novel *Value For Money* with William Fairchild as Ron's co-author. The rewards were negligible and professional satisfaction was lacking. Ron was ready for a change of direction.

From then on Ron would write new plays and film scripts only sporadically.

Ron's last big contribution to the theatre was *Napoleon in Love* which had started life as a novel and was turned into a play for the Pitlochry Festival in 1960. It was a sequel to *The Mayerling Affair* and pandered to Ron's life-long fascination with the emperor which had started when he was sixteen, discovering Lockhart's *Napoleon Bonaparte* on a bookstall. He read it for hours until the kindly bookseller suggested he bought the book.

As a play, *Napoleon In Love* lasted two hours, beginning with the announcement of Napoleon's divorce from Josephine at Fontainebleau. She could not present him with a legitimate heir, a preposition which actually ravaged his conscience more than people imagined. It continues with the description of the first meeting of the eighteen-year-old Marie Louise of Habsburg, whose training for marriage was incomplete to say the least ('but what can one expect of a Habsburg', quipped the author), the grooms matchless experience with women, the Imperial wooing, the birth of the King of Rome and the return of Napoleon from the debacle of 1812.

The size of the cast was a problem which was satisfactorily solved by the 'beating heart' of the Pitlochry Festival, Mr. Kenneth Ireland, who proved excessively tolerant. it was not a conventionally-shaped drama, but a chronicle play presented in a series of scenes, closing with dramatic black-outs. The dialogue incorporated many of the sayings by or about Napoleon which history has transmitted, and it describes the tenderness the emperor was capable of as a lover.

The principal roles were played by Margaret Vines (Josephine), Janet Henfrey (Letizia, Napoleon's mother), John Scarborough (Napoleon) and Judith Conrow (as Marie-Louise).

The *Pitlochry Sunday* commented that 'Mr. Delderfield can be trusted with history' and that out of the three plays reviewed that year, it was ' the one which the company, despite the large casting demands upon it, easily showed up best.'

To contribute to the world premiere of *Napoleon In Love*, Ron wrote an article in which he confessed that he was 'of course an Imperialist' and that his theory was, that had Napoleon triumphed over the autocracies of Europe, the Continent would have been federalised a century ago, and the tragedies of 1914 and 1939 would never have happened. Ron believed that Napoleon was a century ahead of his time, and that what he sought to do in 1806, is being done today – the unification of Europe.

Few people make the connection between the novelist R.F. Delderfield and the first of the *Carry On* films. In fact, *Carry On Sergeant* was based on Ron's play *The Bull Boys*, adapted by him and featuring the young William Hartnell, Bob Monkhouse, Shirley Eaton, Eric Barker, Dora Bryan, Bill Owen, Kenneth Connor, Charles Hawtrey, Kenneth Williams and Hattie Jacques. It was televised a few months before the publication of *The Avenue Saga*.

In 1961, *Stop At A W inner* was turned into a film under the title *On The Fiddle*. In the USA, it was changed to *Operation SNAFU*. It was the first ever film in which Sean Connery starred, together with Alfred Lynch, Cecil Parker, Kathleen Harrison, Eleanor Summerfield, Eric Barker and John Le Mesurier.

It is the story of two heroes, a 'fiddler' and his mate, engaged on using the RAF as an oyster and prising the pearls from it. They find that the opposition are Germans and extricate themselves in a fast-moving tale, ending in a dramatic climax. The foreword read: 'For all the Judies and Erks, who had difficulty in taking the RAF seriously, and particularly for Anne, who seemed to find it all so uproariously funny.'

Anne had been a breath of fresh air during the war years at a dreary camp at Peplow. She had become a good friend to the Delderfields and had always stayed in contact with them after the war.

Once Aboard A Lugger, written years ago, had its world premiere at the Pavilion in Exmouth staged by the ever-loyal Exmouth Players in the presence of Ronald Shiner, the star of *Worm's Eye View* in London, and Ron himself. It was the story of a local fisherman's discovery of gold bullion in a wreck in a West Country bay, owned by the politically ambitious Lord of the Manor; the fisherman contrived to sail away with the loot and the landowner's sister. After the Exmouth flurry, nothing more was heard of the play.

By June 1962, *Worm's Eye View*, which had never really disappeared and was always performed in one provincial theatre or another, was finally on radio on the BBC's 'Saturday Night Theatre'. Ronald Shiner, who had championed the play from the start in 1945, produced it. He had played the main role of Porter in the comedy for three years twice nightly at the Whitehall Theatre and two-and-a-half years at the Comedy, to the delight of the author: 'I couldn't be more pleased,' said Delderfield with glee, to which Ronald Shiner answered: 'Nor me; lumme, I knew at once that *Worm's Eye View* was just my cup of tea. It put me on the map, made me a star. As for the film, it broke all box-office records.'

Listeners had to wait until the 18th June 1964, to hear another one of Ron's plays, *The Offending Hand* in which Jean Lowry is reflecting upon the problems of having a delinquent brother, who constantly threatens the family security. Martin, the father, separated from his wife, is an easy-going, nervous teacher, unable to be strong with his weak-willed son. Prissy, his aunt, who has taken over the mother's role, is being possessive and indulgent towards the problem child. The sister Jean is dating the policeman who had sent the lad to borstal. Eventually, they are forced to conclude that the law-abiding life they had all hoped for him, was not in his nature.

Without being too intrusive into the Delderfield's private life, this play dealt with a problem of their own. Paul had become a difficult boy in his teens, despite of all the love and money lavished on him and his sister. He had found it hard to settle down to a job or profession and very early on in his adolescence developed a dependency problem. He was given money to travel, an antiques' book shop was set up for him, he attended various apprenticeships, but none of them led to a regular lifestyle. He had never come to terms with the fact that his natural mother had given him away for adoption, and he could not acknowledge the difficulties of being an unmarried mother in the 1940s. It seems rather sad to learn that not only was he a cause for worry, but, in later years, after his father's death, May became rather frightened of his temper, when she had lost the protection of her husband. She subsequently moved to live with her daughter Veronica.

At Easter 1969, *A Spark In Judea* was broadcast on the BBC's network all over the world, with a foreword that Ron had taped specially at the Exeter studios.

The very last play, Ron took the trouble to stage was *The Key To The Hut*. The story concerns a man supposed to be a highbrow writer on Lakeland poets who is in fact writing pornographic paperback novels for a Canadian publisher.

The play was performed by the Sidmouth Amateur Dramatic Society, of which Ron was president, at the Manor Pavilion as the climax of the third Sidmouth Drama Festival. It was given a good reception by an enthusiastic first night audience on the 19th May 1970.

Permission for the world premiere to be staged at Sidmouth was given by Mr. Emile Littler, the London impresario, to whom Ron had sold the rights of the play.

Mr. Gene Gerard, a former star of West End musicals, had agreed to direct the production for the society, and the chairman of the Sidmouth Council, Mr. Arthur White, gave a midday sherry party to celebrate the occasion.

By then, Ron had achieved success as a novelist. He realised that his greatest achievement as a playwright had been *Worm's Eye View* and that none of his later plays ever achieved similar success.

ELEVEN

A Thriller and the Swann Saga
(1968 -1971)

Ron is sitting in his study at the Gazebo, a circular-shaped, thatched house, perched on the cliffs at Peak Hill, only a few yards from the family's previous residence. He sighs with relief at the thought that they would never live in an unwieldy big house again.

He looks out of the window, which is shadowed by a huge hedge, obscuring the view out to the sea. He insists that it is left tall. The view is so spectacular; he would never get a chance to concentrate on writing.

He smiles. He has just received a letter from his old RAF friend Dora Haken, who lives now in the area where he has seen his first primrose in 1918: in the woods on the left of Spout Hill between Shirley and Cudham. Then it was a wilderness. He wonders what it looks like now.

He pictures Dora – one of the prettiest Waafs. She seems to remember their time in Hinton-in-the-Hedges as well as he does.

'I must recommend to her to read *On the Fiddle*, he muses, 'she will recognise Hinton in it. Come to think of it, I described every camp I was ever sent to... and it was Sean Connery's first big role when it was filmed.'

The house is quiet now. May has gone shopping, which will result in more antiques joining their huge collection. May has still an eye for a good piece.

Veronica is now 21 and married to a helicopter pilot in the Royal Marines in Singapore. He misses her ebullience, hearing her storm into the house and telling her mother excitedly and breathlessly about her riding adventures.

He also thinks wistfully about Paul, his son, who is attending a farrier's course at Hereford. Ron hopes that the boy will enjoy it and more so, stick to it.

'I must send Dora a photo', Ron decides. He opens the desk drawer, rummages around a pile of pictures and finally takes out the photo of him and his Labrador. 'Haven't I gone bald', he writes on the back and hopes that she remembers him with a fuller head of hair.

Apart from his collection of essays, written from the standpoint of a man in his mid-fifties, called *For my own Amusement*, Ron has immersed himself in writing a thriller, which will come out in June 1968. Ron dedicates *Come Home Charlie And Face Them* to Tom Salmon who suggested a thriller during a BBC interview. It is mainly curiosity that drives Ron to writing in a different genre and, typically for its author, it turns out to be more of a 'why dunnit' than a 'who dunnit'.

Charlie is about an ex-bank clerk in a small Welsh town who robbed his own bank because he hated it. However, as he commits the perfect crime, the book is more concerned with the clerk's psychological problems. Charlie tries first to break out of the futile progression of his life and later to conquer the fears that his rebellion brings. The hero will, in the end, not face anyone because he is incurably ill.

Ron recently declined his first invitation to the United States, where *A Horseman Riding By* and *The Green Gauntlet* have become bestsellers. The first book sold 60,000 hardback copies and 500,000 paperbacks in the States.

Boston University puts his work on the reading list for their English Literature students and requests some of his original manuscripts. After clearing the matter with the Air Ministry, Ron sends various service and note books to their special Collections Department.

Later, these will be followed by manuscripts of his books, television and radio plays, including two unpublished novels called *Big Fish Small Pond* (written ca. 1950) and *The Adventures of Cornet Cavendish* (written 1931/32).

Ron is gratified, because he feels that that part of America has become home to many West County people who have settled in New England.

'It is sad that no approach has ever been made from an English institution,' comments May with a little bitterness.

The other thing which bothers Ron is that he doesn't seem to get a bean for repeats on TV. ITV showed recently the sixth film of his in six months and somehow, 'mechanical rights' in the contract prevent them from paying him royalties.

Spark in Judea is the Easter play of the BBC World Service. However, it is now three years since he has written anything new for the BBC, after they insisted that Josephine, Napoleon's wife, should be a British spy in one of his plays. Ron remembers well the fervour with which he had defended the historically correct ending in favour of the editor's idea.

By the end of 1969, Ron has fallen entirely out of love with television. Back in January 1968, he had expressed his feelings in the *Western Morning News*:

'They won't let me say what I want to say. There is a group of young story editors and their outlook is completely different to mine. Many chaps in my age group want to identify with youth, but I find it not only impossible but undignified. The spectacle of a man of fifty-five, trying to behave like a boy of twenty-one is ridiculous. Nine-tenths of the people in television are terribly afraid of being thought 'square', and this obviates any expression of patriotism. They behave like women who refuse to admit that they remember the silent movies!'

Ron is also annoyed at his defeat at the hands of Plymouth City Council, who turned down his offer of a plaque on Plymouth Hoe to commemorate Napoleon's visit there aboard the 'Bellerophon' in 1815. Ron can not suppress a giggle thinking of the irony that he will appear on French television in a programme about Napoleon's connections with England. He has already thought about the comments he is going to make in front of the camera and can picture himself pointing proudly to the ship's mooring on the Hamoaze.

He picks up a brand-new volume of his most recent book on Napoleon, *Imperial Sunset: The Fall of Napoleon 1813-14*. The book ends with Napoleon being sent into exile; Waterloo was yet to come.

Ron opens the cover and reads the dedication to a fellow enthusiast, Sir Arthur Bryant.

According to the critic William McElwee, it is a remarkably readable book and Ron remembers the *Boston Globe*'s comment which said: 'Delderfield writes with gusto, enriching his narrative with innumerable citations from the memoirs and documents of the period and shrewd observations of characters.'

The Library Journal is even more generous with praise: 'The facts, the human element, the course of history are all here told in accurate detail by a master historian.'

Words like these warm Ron's heart and make him glow. It recompenses the author for 'living almost exclusively with shadows and shadows that fade after publication day.'
(*This England*, spring 1969).

Being patriotic has always been important to Ron. He wants everyone to take pride in being British. It maddens him if people go around apologising for it. He is convinced that the British are the kindest and most tolerant nation in the world.

'I would sooner have that said about us than anything else!' he mumbles to himself.

He remembers a recent interview which was fun. Someone asked him which alternative life he would consider to that of an author, and he surprised himself how quickly he found three very acceptable alternatives:

The life of an English or history master at a small public school;

A professional soldier in an easygoing regiment;

A parson in a remote rural parish, preferably one bordering on the coastline.

He would not like anything exacting or depriving him of privacy, and he has come to appreciate predictability socially and financially, not leading to enormous fortunes, but the security of the proverbial roof over his head, companionship of colleagues and close contact with the young.

He would not be a school master orientated towards examination results. In a way, a position such as he has in mind, leaving him the choice of syllabus and exercising his own brand or rather lack of discipline, probably doesn't exist. He dreams of teaching and discussing Wilfred Owen, Cervantes, Palmerston, The War of the Roses, Aldington's *Death of a Hero*, Barbara Tuchman's *August 1914*, rather less the politics of Kings and Queens, but more about their human strengths and failings. 'The 'B' roads of English verse and the bypaths of history are what I would follow. *Kidnapped* would be a must, I would skip *King Lear* and I would end the day with brandy and soda, Liszt and Rubenstein for company.'

As a soldier, he would not want to be a hero, but spend his time skylarking in the mess as a subaltern, at polo matches or in pleasant garrison towns and he would finally retire to Budleigh Salterton. 'There is no less offensive way of loafing from cradle to grave!' he muses.

The third temptation would be the rectory, with a big open fireplace and walls filled with leather-bound books. He would not put the fear of the Devil into his parishioners, but he would potter among them during the week and enquire about their welfare on Sundays, all within five hundred yards of the fireside, pretending to be in deep contemplation when called to tea, ready to wade into the crumpets.

'Come to think of it, I met just such a man recently,' he grins as he puts *Imperial Sunset* back on the book shelve behind him.

Ron is in the middle of creating a new canvas, his biggest yet: a four volume saga, of which his readers expect the first volume, *God Is An Englishman,* by March 1970.

He doesn't want anything to interrupt the flow of his writing and he refuses to leave his beloved Devon simply to get into slinging matches with TV companies. A short trip to the Investiture of the Prince of Wales, to which the *Western Morning News* has sent him, is enough travelling for one year.

Ron explains in an interview in September 1969, that his new saga is an attempt to analyse how Britain came to play such a dominant role in the destiny of the human race.

It is a huge canvas stretching over three generations of the Swann family. Adam Swann, a cavalry officer during the Indian mutiny, not only survives the action, but is also presented by fate with a precious find, a broken casket which contains a string of rubies. This would become the capital on which Swann On Wheels, a string of road haulage depots, where the new railways were at their weakest, would be founded. It is the birth of an entrepreneur and it gives the reader a vivid picture of the England of their great-grandfathers.

Henrietta, the spirited and idealistic daughter of a ruthless mill-owner, will provide the love interest in the story, and the numerous depot managers give ample opportunity for descriptions of human nature – which Ron is so good at.

Ron has always been writing six hours a day, seven days a week, but during this period of his life, 1967 to 1972 it seems as if the floodgates of his matured creativity have been opened.

The Swann Saga is planned to run to four volumes. It is a lot of close print. *God Is an Englishman* alone counts 687 pages, but now Ron's publishers, Hodder & Stoughton, ride with him on the wave of success without fear of a colossal disaster.

The role of editing the hundreds of pages, Ron has churned out, falls to Robin Denniston, who has to keep up with the steady flow of manuscripts handed in by Ron. With the success of *A Horseman Riding By* the public has proven that it is ready for a jolly good, long read, and no-one dares to discourage the author any longer.

When the first volume of the Swann saga is published in March 1970, the critics fall over themselves with enthusiasm.

The Nottingham Guardian Journal writes: 'A wholly engrossing novel, one that must be counted as among the very best of its kind. Certainly Mr Delderfield has never done better.'

The Birmingham Evening Mail praises the book as 'exciting, absorbing and thoroughly readable.'

'Enthralling, irresistible and a masterpiece,' added others.

'He writes with such beautiful, cartographical neatness,' applauds the *Sunday Times* and continues: ' Anybody can start a period novel well, with chapter titles and twirls; Delderfield is among the few that can draw you all the way through close print.'

May loves the story, the characters of Adam and Henrietta Swann, their idyllic, grand house which they discover by chance – 'squatting between the two dark spurs of woodland, moonlight casting long shadows across the pantiled roof, looking like a self-indulgent old man, snuggling under the blankets, with the silvered chimney-pots showing as a few tufts of hair above the counterpane.' May loves the name 'Tryst', they gave to the house, the much-neglected seat previously of the noble families of Conyer and Collingwood, 'off the long slope of a dust road that wound its way between gorse-studded hills, then down the sharp descent of Spout Hill towards the open country beyond Addington.'

The publication of *God Is An Englishman* is followed by a promotional journey of three thousand miles for seven weeks, covering the routes of most of Adam Swann's regional depots. The trip includes three literary luncheons, five booksellers' cocktail parties, twelve radio tape recordings for home and overseas, two television appearances and eighteen press interviews, all accompanied by rather inclement winter weather.

This trip confirms Ron in his belief that 'the face of England changes, but the soul is much the same; patience, enterprise, ingenuity, a deep concern for law and order, neighbourliness, sanity, self-respect and, above all, a quality of tolerance that does not flourish anywhere else on earth.'

One change, however, gives him great pleasure: the army of efficient young women, who lead him through interviews and recordings with a sure, but well-manicured hand, without ever getting flustered or unable to cope, which suggests to him that 'had Adam Swann had the good sense of recruiting a dozen women for his depots, he might have been a millionaire by 1870'.

Ron has always liked women, and he absolutely believes that 'if Parliament was made up entirely of officials picked from Women's Institutes and Towns Women's Guilds, we should solve most of our social and economic problems in a single session. They have a way of sifting the relevant from the inconsequential and are not much given to self glorification.'

An exhausted Ron is greeted on his return in mid-May by a performance of his play *The Key to the Hut* staged by his old friends of the Sidmouth Amateur Dramatic Society as the climax of the Sidmouth Drama Festival. It is a world premier and everyone is very proud that their president has agreed for the play to be presented in front of a home audience.

The story exposes a highbrow author as a fraud, who supposedly writes about Lakeland poets, but secretly churns out pornographic paperback novels for a Canadian publisher. The entire Sidmouth cast is thrilled to be directed by the West End musical star Gene Gerrard and a huge crowd of locals turns out to mark the occasion.

Meanwhile, Ron's admiring readership is impatient for the *Swann* saga to continue. The sequel is published in the following year with the title *Theirs Was The Kingdom*. It takes the story forward from the Zulu war to Queen Victoria's Golden Jubilee. The network of haulage depots expands to Scotland and Ireland and the large family is growing up: one son will be a professional soldier, another a pioneer of motor transport, the adopted daughter crusading against injustices done to young working-class girls – all that in front of the background of the Victorian kaleidoscope.

Ron dedicates this even larger volume to his good friend Eric McKenzie, who had first worked for Hodder & Stoughton in Edinburgh before being promoted and sent to London. Eric has often accompanied Ron on his promotional travels and is 'as enterprising as any Swann salesman and cheerleader extraordinaire.'

'Your families are always rumbustious', May remarks laughingly. 'Look at Adam and Henrietta and their brood, never a dull day.'

'With my up-bringing what else can I write about,' Ron chuckles, remembering his father who was irrepressible to his last day.

'It was nice of Robert Delderfield to take the trouble of tracing our origins and drawing up our family tree.'

He ruffles through the papers in his in-tray. He finally pulls out a letter he has recently received from his distant relative.

'Fancy tracing our family so far back: Joseph Tanner, born in 1891 and we might even descend from the Huguenots.'

Ron sits back in his chair and sighs with satisfaction.

TWELVE

A London Childhood
(1912 – 1918)

Ronald Frederick Delderfield was born on February 12th 1912 in the London Borough of New Cross, two months before the Titanic sank.

He had three brothers: Ewart, named after old Mr. Delderfield's hero Gladstone, but had died of scarlet fever when he was six; William, born in 1901, who missed being a Victorian by twenty-one days; and Eric, who was born two-and-a-half years before little Ronnie.

The family had first lived at 58 Reverdy Road in Central London, but had moved to a more open neighbourhood in Waller Road in New Cross, to accommodate their growing numbers.

William James Delderfield, Ronnie's father, was, heavily involved in politics and needed to be closer to the Council Offices, so they moved back to South-East London and occupied a large, roomy house with a stable yard at 144 Fort Road, which the five of them shared with a deaconess lodger.

William James Delderfield, the head of the household, had been born in Bermondsey in 1873 into an old Bermondsey family of leather-dressers. As a boy, he carried a man's hot dinner for a penny a day. He was short, extremely active and independent and had a vast, disorganised store of general knowledge. His first job was with a Tower Bridge tea importer at thirteen-and-a-half, by which time he was a seasoned adult.

Until the age of twenty-three, Ronnie's father followed the family tradition of leather-dressing, but then became a clerk and market attendant to a Bermondsey firm in the Meat Trade for fourteen years, and later a salesman on Smithfield Meat Market for another firm for a further three years.

In 1903, he had been elected to the Council with a record number of votes as the only Progressive. He had also been a Deacon of the Rouel Road Congregational Church for twelve years, a Superintendent of its Band of Hope and a Superintendent for its Sunday school for sixteen years.

He was considered the most fearless of speakers, vigorous, humorous, witty, with a biting sarcasm aimed at his opponents. *The Bermondsey Liberal Monthly* reported: 'He may occasionally appear wild in his utterances, but he rarely misses the point of argument and his earnestness cannot be misunderstood. He has plenty of lung-power and generally has the best of the battle, when the other side endeavour to howl him down!' It also acknowledged that 'Mr. Delderfield is moved by the belief that he lives for a specific purpose, and is sufficiently unselfish to devote a large portion of his leisure to try to teach the next generation better modes of life, imbuing them with principles of a higher morality. Today, he stands high in the estimation of those who know him.'

An eccentric and richly comic character he may have been, but to a child, he was an often absentee father, who on his returns must have hit the family like a whirlwind. He was passionate about his heroes: Gladstone, the Suffragettes, Charlie Chaplin (because he had refused American citizenship), Lincoln, Livingstone and Robbie Burns. He further admired Christian souls like the missionary Mary Slessor of Calebar and James Chalmers, who had been a missionary, but had been killed and eaten by Papuans. The house was cluttered with their busts and their huge and often read biographies.

In spite of the fact that Ronnie rarely set eyes on his volatile father, except when he marched his sons to Chapel on Sundays and nudged them fiercely 'to sing up', and a fortnightly annual holiday at the seaside, the little boy adored him and thought him quite infallible.

While working at Smithfield's, Mr. Delderfield would get up at 4 a.m., return at 1 p.m., go to bed until 5 p.m., during which mother would not have him roused, even if the household had been on fire; he would then have a hasty meal at 5.30 p.m. and rush out of the house to the Council at 6 p.m., when Ronnie was off to bed. Mondays to Saturdays, father was a rip-roaring extrovert, but on Sundays, it was as well to keep out of his way because, for some reason the children never understood, a heavy and hopeless gloom engulfed him.

This might have had something to do with his wife, who hated cooking and produced Sunday lunch with scant grace, making heavy weather of it until it was on the table.

Mrs. Delderfield, *née* Alice Jones, was born in 1876 as the only daughter of a Welshman, whose family had set out from Devil's Bridge, Aberystwyth, in the eighteen-fifties to seek their fortune in

London. Her father worked all his life in a tea warehouse opposite Tower Bridge. She attended one of the first London elementary schools and her standard of education – although she had gone out to work at thirteen – frequently astonished her children. She knew many of Shakespeare's plays and loved Dickens, about whose characters she would talk engagingly to the boys.

She bought all the classics for the children in abridged form, so they never suffered from literary indigestion, but were grateful to her for the common sense in leading them softly – but none the less firmly – into the embrace of Scott, Defoe, Swift, Kingsley, Bunyan and George Eliot.

Before her marriage, Mrs. Delderfield had been in business in Rye Lane, and the despotism of the late-Victorian drapery trade did not daunt her one bit. She was a living-in shop assistant and was dedicated to money-making. Bullying customers would rather amuse than intimidate her.

No wonder then, that even after marriage, she was essentially a business woman who was bored by household chores. She saw to it that the boys learnt manners and could get very annoyed at the loss of a good shirt. It took her several years to get over the tortured springs of the drawing room sofa, that had been broken on Ronnie's eleventh birthday by a house full of rumbustious guests.

In a way, she was an unemotional woman who watched over her children's education and health, but once they were out of sight, she washed her hands of them.

It was just as well that she was reserved and able to balance her husband's mercurial temperament. Politically, she was High Tory and cancelled out father's Radical vote at every Parliamentary election between 1918 and 1953. She would go to evening services at the Congregationalists church to worship, while the rest of the family went with father to morning service.

Ronnie grew up to accept unending yet jovial conflict as a natural state of affairs accompanying marriage and home-life.

There were also six aunts, sisters of his father, who were temperamentally very much alike, true Cockneys, but who physically had very little in common.

Maud and Ada, always wearing black and green respectively, were generously built. Maud was the superintendent of the Municipal Baths, who after being widowed worked her way up by sheer force of character. Harriet was the barnstormer, ebullient, puncturing the family's balloons of self-esteem. Emma, the eldest, appeared rarely, probably because of her large family, but Auntie Nell was the wittiest, gentlest and most kind-hearted of the lot.

The boys always enjoyed their aunts' visits, because they were six star-performers, each trying to corner the attention of their audience, and not least, giving them pennies and sixpences for their piggy banks.

In fact, Ronnie and Eric shared a piggy bank for Christmas and seaside money. It was unsuccessful, as it soon turned out, because Eric had an extraordinarily acquisitive streak and always spent every penny of his share on the first day of the holiday, so that he had to borrow constantly from the younger brother. Years later, the grown-up Ron would dedicate one of his books to Eric with the inscription: 'What about my Bognor money? What about my Felixstowe money? What about my Shanklin money, diverting to you, but galling me more every year!' Eric was to remain preoccupied with money matters all his life.

The family's annual August holiday used to be a hit and miss affair, planned by Mr. Delderfield with the help of the Southern railway Holiday Guide and without consultation of the family.

The first one was at Bognor, where they stayed at the 'Kia Ora' lodgings; it was memorable only because Ronnie nearly drowned, had not his eldest brother Bill saved him.

The second holiday at the hotel Glenavon in Shanklin was preceded by various lectures in table manners by Mrs. Delderfield, who promised a prize of one shilling, which was promptly won by the ever acquisitive Eric. Ronnie didn't mind much, because he had fallen in love for the first time with a little brunette, who wore a print frock and had plaits tied with ribbons.

It was followed by an ill-fated series of holidays – one at Felixstowe, where his parents took the boys on a boat to see the lighthouse; this trip made Ronnie so violently ill with chronic earache that he had to be taken to a doctor.

Then there was the holiday at Swanage, where the lodgings were awful and where a circuit round the Isle of Wight brought on more seasickness, which turned out to be the outbreak of scarlet fever. Ronnie had to be taken to hospital where he had to stay until October. As this was a very lonely and boring time, he took to reading his first book, *A Peep Behind the Scenes*, which, he insisted later, had prejudiced him for life in favour of sentimental writing.

The next holiday at Colwyn Bay was pleasant, but marred by broken glasses which gave him a distorted view of North Wales thereafter. The family decided that he had become their holiday jinx.

Ronnie's eldest brother, Bill, whom he first remembered as a grave-eyed, knicker-bockered sixteen-year- old and who taught him how to tell the time by the kitchen clock, was a natural spendthrift. He also frequently borrowed money from little Ronnie, who was known to be very careful, even miserly – and who became the butt of family jokes when he tried to call in his debts, of which he kept detailed accounts.

Bill disappeared from the family's life when he ran away and signed on as a steward on a merchant ship, under-age and against his father's will. In the winter of 1916/17, he sailed with a submarine, but turned up only weeks afterwards having been torpedoed off Falmouth and set adrift in an open boat. This did not deter him, and he signed on straight away again, bound for South America and West Africa.

After demobilisation, he worked as a butcher in Peckham for a year, but that was too humdrum for him and he announced that he would be off to Australia. There he stayed, married an Australian girl named Freda, joined the police and finally became Police Commissioner of Tasmania, after an Act of Parliament made it possible for him as a foreigner to take up the post.

Ronnie never ceased to admire his eldest brother in spite of not seeing him for thirty-five years. Things happened to Bill in a way they never happened to the rest of the family. However, he remained a most dependable and solid man. Ronnie and Bill were to write to each other frequently for the rest of their lives, and once an author, Ron thanked his brother 'for thirty years of encouragement' by dedicating his novel *The Avenue Goes To War* to him.

Ronnie was only two years old when the first World War started. During raids, his father would not budge to find shelter, while the boys were wrapped in eiderdowns by their mother and carried downstairs to the kitchen, where they were given Smithfield Market order pads to scribble upon. This was meant to take their minds off the Zeppelins.

As the war went on, Ronnie joined a State infant school in Bermondsey, but his mother's nerves weakened more with every raid, so that he started to dread walking with her in the street, because she would burst into tears the moment someone spoke to her. To relieve the stress, the family went on weekend -trips to the country, visiting aunts at Hounslow and Leigh in Kent. The countryside was a great discovery for a child that had been brought up in the asphalt and concrete jungle of London. He gradually began to hate having to return to Ford Road.

And then, one fine spring morning in 1918, Mr. Delderfield announced that they would all move to the then still rural and peaceful Addiscombe on the Kent/Surrey border, where an uncle had recently bought a house in Ashbourton Avenue.

Ronnie was delighted!

The family tree drawn up by Ron.

122

THIRTEEN

To Serve Them All My Days
(1971-1972)

'I wish Parliament would introduce legislation against those who persist in the archaic notion that to beat children is to improve them', Ron writes in one of his essays, collected in the volume *Overture for Beginners*, and continues: 'It is a system of instruction based on fear which is bound to be utterly unsuccessful.'

He has always had a very clear idea of the role of ideal teachers: 'Their aim would have nothing to do with demands of examinations of any kind, but to turn out decent fathers, husbands, mothers and wives. They would be more counsellors than teachers and would let history and English literature do their work for them, the ethos of which might even filter through to the nation.'

In February 1971, he dedicates a school story to his 'friend and colleague of the book-world', Hodder & Stoughton's Robin Denniston. It is not so much concerned with the fate of one school master, but with a whole array of characters, masters and pupils in a private boarding school. In his disclaimer, Ron admits that this story is very much a portrayal of West Buckland School.

He hasn't changed the location and the characters are an amalgam of all the schoolmasters and pupils he had met in the six schools, he had been sent to between 1917 and 1929. Out of those six, he had loathed the first five.

The working title of this school story is at one stage *The Low Mr. Chips* indicating that it is supposed to be a kind of sequel to *Good Bye, Mr. Chips*. It is finally published as *To Serve Them All My Days* and depicts not only the country emerging from the Great War, but an educational system that is in dire need of humanising.

Ron sets out to create the character of a teacher as a figurehead. David Powlett-Jones, a miner's son, who has survived Passchendaele, finds a job as an unqualified history teacher in a small public school on Exmoor. He soon displays that rare talent to guide the boys effortlessly with kindness, wisdom and enthusiasm. Through his eyes and his heart, the readers witness generations of schoolboys entering the school, engaging in its activities, taking its ethos away with them into adult life and returning to it as old boys or as parents of new boys. David leads his pupils and colleagues with love and sympathy as one who has suffered and comprehends the suffering of others.

Ron and May practise what they preach.

'We are sparse with discipline, but very good with love,' May insisted whenever the children gave them problems, particularly Paul, who for a long time didn't settle.

Both children were showered with love and attention, but it didn't seem to make any difference to Paul. He was allowed to travel and on his return, various small businesses were set up for him, but it took him years to find inner peace and his niche in life. Ron sighs. They have done their best for the children; no-one could have been more well-meaning, generous, tolerant and kind.

Next, Ron is engrossed in writing the third volume of the Swann saga. The triumphs and disasters of the Swann family find their conclusion in *Give Us This Day*, which followed them into the times when the motor engine took over from the horse, when the troubles in Ireland began and the first signs of a World War One appeared.

The success of the saga promises to be enormous, and the interest from the United States surpasses all his expectations, where it is the 'Choice of the Month' of the Literary Guild of America even before its publication.

Ron finally succumbs and accepts an invitation of his American publishers Simon Schuster travel to New York at the end of September 1970. He boards the QE2 liner with great misgivings, having been fed a rather violent picture of that continent by the press and television for years. What he finds is enormous hospitality, luxury, offers to write for newspapers on the first day of his arrival, and invitations to two television shows, eight radio programmes and twenty press interviews.

He is invited to two glamorous parties without anyone bullying or harrying him during the two weeks he is staying. He is utterly overwhelmed by the sincere and warm welcome extended to him and the thoughtfulness with which they treat him.

The Americans he meets are genuinely interested in England, 'as if it were an elderly uncle whose vast experience qualifies him in some way to advise and counsel an enterprising young nephew, who finds himself suddenly saddled with being in charge of the entire Western World.'

He is tremendously proud when shown the separate collection of his manuscripts and note books in the Special Collections Department at Boston University and promises to send more.

'What a treat!' Ron enthuses on his return and adds wistfully: 'I am only sorry that I have not availed myself of it many years before.'

During his absence, his unashamedly autobiographical school story, *To Serve Them All My Days*, has done well. Ron remembers his days at West Buckland School, high up on Exmoor, with great fondness.

His old school friend, Harold 'Romeo' Boyer reminds him: 'You used to act a bit of a fool, pretending you were something of a weakling. And you did get away with it!'

'Romeo' was two years older than Ron and went on to become a prefect and later returned as a housemaster.

Ron often turns up at the school to speak to the boys, loaf through the classrooms and stroll across the playing fields, just as he had done as a pupil.

'West Buckland School has this curious fascination for him,' confirms Harold. 'Ron is always coming back, looking for anecdotes and material that he can put in his books. As a youngster, Dido was a kind and gentle boy, one with a sense of humour.'

It hadn't started that way when Ron was taken by his father to join this remote boarding school on Exmoor. Ron had been among the pupils of his previous school, The Grange in Exmouth, who were supposed to be involved in the 'Brickyard Kissing' incident. They were at first all expelled only to be re-instated after the culprits had been found.

By then, Ron's father had lost his patience. He was less angry with Ron than with the school. It only confirmed his intuitive misgivings; he had never believed in the success of co-education and Ron's mother was determined to have her son turned into a gentleman.

FOURTEEN

West Buckland
(1926 – 1928)

On April, the 18th 1926, Mr. Delderfield senior took his son as far as Exeter and then put him on a train to the fringe of Exmoor. It passed the stations of Wiveliscombe, Bampton, Morebath, Vencross, Anstey, Molland and South Molton, before it called at Filleigh Station, where all the boys alighted. They then trudged up the hill all together to a huddle of grey buildings, a kind of stone-faced Crystal Palace. It was called West Buckland School, and would become Ronnie's last and most favourite school and home for two-and-a-half years.

In those days, it accommodated two hundred boys and promoted toughness and a Spartan atmosphere, but also kindness, spirit and patriotism.

In 1963, encouraged by his old pal 'Romeo' Boyer, Ron collected and assembled reminiscences of Old Buckland Boys in a thin volume, called *Tales Out Of School*.

It is permeated by the affection these ex-pupils still felt for their school years after they had left it, and reflected the fun they had had during their school days there.

On the day of arrival, Ron, now fourteen years of age, was straight away taken in hand by a sixth-former who posted him outside the headmaster's office. 'Ernie' Harris, who ruled West Buckland for twenty-seven years and who played Rugby regularly with the boys when he was sixty-three, welcomed him warmly and allocated him to 'Dormy Six'. He had to share it with Morton, an Exeter hotelier's son, Dean, a farmer's son and Commander Chard.

A little later it emerged that Ron and his housemaster, Cartner, a trench veteran, could not get on. On the advice of an older pupil, Ron approached 'Ernie', hesitantly, because in his past experiences headmasters had been fearsome and unapproachable. But 'Ernie' was different; he listened and said simply: 'Borrow the handcart, get your things and make a fresh start in the Brereton dormitory. You are a bit wild but there is nothing basically wrong with you!'

Ron desperately wanted to conform to this school. Maybe it was a legacy of his mother who, all her life, had looked for peaceful anonymity and never found it at the side of her husband. However, Ron's strong Cockney accent and a tendency to dramatise everyday situations, gave him the label of buffoon, which carried with it a certain gratuitous popularity.

Ron soon acquired a nickname, like everyone else. They called him 'Dido', after he had chosen to read the part of Queen Dido in a Latin class on the Iliad. His class mates fell about laughing as the bespectacled Cockney ploughed his way through the text in the most dreadful accent.

More so than ever, English and History became Ron's favourite subjects. He was very fortunate indeed to have dedicated and capable teachers like Sam Howells, his English master, a sandy-haired, slightly-built and rather florid man with a superiority over his colleagues and their subjects, in spite of the fact that he had no degree. Sam Howells introduced Ron's class to *The Rose and the Ring*, *Westward Ho*, *Don Quixote*, *The Heroes* and *Frossart's Chronicles of England, France and Spain*, Scott's *Tales of a Grandfather* and Froude's *English Seamen of the Sixteenth Century*.

Sam was fastidious, drank gin, smoked fifty cigarettes a day and couldn't pronounce the letter 'r', which he replaced by a 'w', 'but by God, how that man could teach!'.

Sam became headmaster of West Buckland School just before the war until his unquiet death of lung cancer in 1952. The adult Ron would always remember him with great fondness: 'He was severe, frigid, touchy, didactic and self-opinionated with a gift for savage irony, but I learnt more about life from him than from any of the highbrow teachers and churchmen I met later in life.'

West Buckland School's staff consisted of eccentrics.

There was Adalbert Taylor, known as 'Judy', a more dignified version of the famous Mr. Chips, a Victorian through and through, who had an almost fanatical passion for order and neatness, regimentation and accuracy. He usually wore a cap on his bald head and forestalled any chuckles by pointing out that, when the boys reached his age, they, too, would need protection against Exmoor draughts.

'Judy' taught mathematics and carpentry, in both of which Ron was hopeless and would be called to order as 'The Prrrrince of Fooools.'

'Bouncer', whose proper name was Billy Bouncer, was the headmaster's brother. He was also the vicar of West Buckland and an excellent teacher of religion, which was a dreadful subject to teach under the circumstances. However, he managed to keep order with the boys by dishing out punishments without being particular whether he punished the culprit or not.

A young teacher, called Armstrong 'Legweak', had a terrible time and stayed only two terms.

Mr. Fry was a sandy little man with a dry sense of humour.

Mr. Darvil, a dapper man, was the life and soul of the School O.T.C.

Mr. Rogers was plagued by old age and short sight. The boys would play terrible tricks on him and, with his 'Be silent boy!', he would invoke even more noise and shouts of 'it wasn't me, Sir!'

'Watto', Mr. Watson, the Music master for many years, had a daughter called Nora, who subsequently married Bellot, the popular Latin teacher, a feast of gossip for the boys.

It was a Spartan environment. On winter mornings, the boys had to break the ice on their washing bowls. The food was stodgy, showed little variation and was supplemented by bi-weekly orders to the tuck shop, plus pasties and tarts sold after chapel on Sundays by a neighbouring farmer's wife. The boys would jostle after an unseemly hasty exit from church in front of Mrs. Stanbury's window to purchase their treats. Only the sixth-formers were allowed into her parlour in front of an apple-log fire, munching away for all to see.

Breakfast consisted of porridge with lumps and dripping toast, on Tuesdays enhanced by an egg, on Thursdays by a fishcake and on Saturdays by one lonely sausage. Lunches were equally uninspiring and consisted of thin slices of beef, boiled potatoes and soggy and eternal cabbage, with a hard-baked cake or tart to follow. Dinner was at 6 p.m., scrape and sugarless tea was all there was, with bread and butter to be given to prefects only for supper.

The school employed a barber who came every six to seven weeks to cut the boys' hair. By then, they could hardly see from under their long fringes, but resembled more a bunch of convicts after the 'tonsorial artist' had finished with them.

There were traditions, the boys remembered well: the clapping in of rugger teams after matches; the mopping up of Whitsun Reunion delicacies on the next day by Fifth and Sixth-Formers; the singing good-nights between dormitories after lights out on the last night of term; the one feast per term for which the senior pupils collected the basic sixpence-a-week pocket money with due pressure; the theatre performances of which some were more disastrous than others, including the actors' feathered costumes going up in flames and Ron nearly freezing to death as a nurse maid, tripping over his gown and falling down a flight of seventeen stone stairs!

Perhaps the most memorable of all was Ron's own play, *Murder in the Pulpit*, appropriately written out of boredom during Sunday church services. When it was performed by the school, the author's instructions were taken quite literally, so that the actors had to be pulled apart to avoid a disaster.

On Sundays, half-holidays and summer evenings, the boys at West Buckland were allowed to roam within and without bounds. Ron loved mooching about the quad, hands in his pockets, 'cocking an ear for the shouts and the sensual snick of ball on blade in the sports field, poking about in the linen room in search of grey, worsted socks, or loping down from Forty Beeches surrounded by panting scuffling humanity.' 'Romeo' Boyer shared those feelings with Ron without having to communicate them. They remained very close friends for the rest of their lives, long after 'Romeo' had become a prefect and later still, a housemaster at West Buckland.

It was not always entirely romantic at West Buckland. There was the Sunday drill, invented by a fiendish Fifth-Former for the first- year boys, during which, according to a series of couplets, they had to perform certain tasks:

LAST SUNDAY BUT TWELVE
NEW KIDS RAVE TO DELVE...

which meant digging and filling in holes along the plantation, or

LAST SUNDAY BUT FOUR
NEW KIDS SCRUB THE FLOOR...

using a tooth brush and tooth paste, which was thoroughly supervised by the tormentors.

Ninging, the courtship of younger boys by seniors, was another peculiar custom.

Ron did not get involved, because he was rather more interested in courting girls. During his holidays he was forever falling in love with somebody or other. For a while, he pursued his courtship of a fluffy, green-eyed girl called Edna, whom he took to the pictures when he was at home. When that relationship fizzled out, he replaced her by Karen, whom he had met in the Easter holidays. She was blond, rather petit and solemn. Her letters from her boarding school somewhere in the north of London were, however, after a while disappointing, because they consisted more of gossip than of romantic declarations and oaths.

Alf Gaite, who was also a new pupil, advised Ron to select a sport before anyone else chose one for him. Ronnie, who had always disliked organised games, selected cross-country running. It was considered quite important at West Buckland and was not as over-crowded as other disciplines. Ron enjoyed jogging through the unspoilt countryside, paced by another pupil, Bill Askham. The annual cross-country events like the run of 'the North-West', 'The Long', 'The Bray', 'The Tuck' and the most testing of the public school year, 'The Exmoor', gave Ron a rare opportunity to gain a few house points by plodding along and just finishing the course. During training, there was the added advantage that the boys could stock up with pasties and custard tarts at nearby farms.

Alf Gaite also taught Ron that nice clothes improved self-confidence. Consequently, Ron asked after his first term for a double-breasted suit and Oxford 'Bags', which delighted his mother no end.

Requests directed at his father were not received with the same enthusiasm. When asking if he should join the headmaster's confirmation class and the Officers Training Corps, his father was not altogether pleased. As a Liberal, he was suspicious of any kind of militarism, but young Ron won the argument by pointing out that he would be considered to be a weak-kneed frowster if he did not enlist like everyone else.

The confirmation classes were, however, declined as 'facted idolatry'. At least Ron could now join the OTC. It turned out not to be all plain sailing: the sergeant-major was fond of comparing Ronnie's efforts to those of a snared and pregnant duck, and the entire Corps was happier when Ron took over the cymbals and kettledrums, which he clanged happily for the rest of his time at West Buckland.

World War One had claimed the lives of a considerable number of Old Boys. This was brought home to Ron on November 11th 1926, when he attended his first armistice service which was held beside the memorial cross, given by surviving Old Boys.

The Head, Ernie Harries, held a short speech about West Buckland casualties, almost all of whom he had known personally as boys. Ron was standing close to him and noticed that, when the bugler sounded the 'Last Post', tears were streaming down Ernie's cheeks.

The near disastrous performance of Ronnie's first play, *Murder In The Pulpit*, was followed by his attempts at writing pornographic crime stories, all in all about fifteen of them. This endeared him to the Upper Fifth, who kept asking for more.

He also tried his hand at erotic science fiction; these were all set in America and again, very popular with the older boys. Unfortunately, they ended up being hurriedly stuffed into a biscuit tin and buried in a rabbit hole in the school grounds, where they might still lie today.

The teachers never discovered what young Delderfield was writing, but were aware that he thought it unnecessary to follow any subjects – including mathematics and all the sciences – that had nothing to do with his chosen career: He was going to be a writer!

So, when the question arose whether he should join the Sixth Form, he was quite happy to return home and to enrol at a commercial college in Exeter instead. After all, his father wanted him to work at his newspaper, *The Exmouth Chronicle*, and, typically of the young Ron, it was not necessary to waste any thought or worry on his future. He favoured to live from day to day.

Ron and his brother Eric were both roped into working for *The Exmouth Chronicle*, the local newspaper, their father had bought. Eric had been sent to gain experience as an apprentice printer in London and Somerset, while Ron enjoyed himself at the Commercial College in Exeter, where the vast majority of pupils were girls.

In fact, he was only one of three male students. This inevitably opened new insights to him, after having lived in the extraordinary seclusion of West Buckland School. He found it very hard to concentrate on the subjects he was supposed to learn, namely shorthand, typing and book-keeping. He took to shorthand reasonably well and learnt to type, but book-keeping was brushed aside as uninteresting.

Particular distractions were caused by the blond Edna, the coquette Muriel with an Eton crop, the freckled Jacqueline and Barbara, whose mind was more on repairing her make-up than on Mr. Pitman's theories. Ron even managed to fall in love with Stella, their nineteen-year old instructress, but had to share her attentions with the other two chaps.

While attending the Commercial College, Ron lived at home with his parents and spent a good deal of his time travelling from Exmouth to Exeter. On his journeys, he read poetry, which soon bored him; so he thought he might try Shakespeare. However, it was in the various volumes of *Famous Plays Of The Year* by a firm named Gollancz, that he discovered much more easy-to-read playwrights. This brought him to the conclusion that it must be a piece of cake to write plays.

On Saturdays, when there was no college, his father expected him to do 'real' work as a layer-in at the *Chronicle*. This meant, folding the paper's pages in the correct sequence all Friday afternoon, evening and before Saturday morning breakfast.

The *Chronicle* sold in those days around three thousand copies per week and Ron was paid a weekly allowance of five shillings.

Ron spent the little leisure time that was left often in Mr. Appleby's second-hand bookshop in company of his old school friend Vic Whitworth. One book made a particular impact on him and set off his life-long interest in the Napoleonic era: it was Lockart's *The Life of Napoleon*. Very soon, his collection of books about this historic epoch would occupy three shelves in his private library. Maron de Marbot became a kind of patron saint to him.

In later life, Ron would carry five favourite books with him wherever he went. They were: Stevenson's *Treasure Island*, the second volume of Carlyle's *French Revolution*, Mark Twain's *Huckleberry Finn*, Baron de Marbot's *Memoirs*, in translation by A.J. Butler, and Helen Ashton's *Doctor Serecold*. He was also very fond of John Betjeman's *Collected Verse*, the *Oxford Book of English Verse* and last, but not least the Bible. Each of these, in their own way, had instilled in him the urge and desire to spin yarns for a living; 'any other way of spending my days would seem bleak beyond the realm of thought,' he would say with feeling.[6]

Sometimes, Ron would travel with friends up to London, where he proved to be as prone to accidents as during childhood family holidays.

On one occasion, his friends had refused to climb up the Monument, but Ron, wanting to view the capital from above, insisted on going up by himself. Enjoying the Olympian view of the Metropolis and feeling rather sorry for the miserable little pigmies crawling around at the base, he felt tempted to find out how long a piece of paper

6. R.F. Delderfield read poetry all his life. He believed that Shakespeare had written his plays to be watched not read.

would take to flutter from this great height to the ground. He dropped a bus ticket through the guard rails and, in order to keep its flight in view, he pushed his head through the bars. Seconds later, it became clear to him that his head had got stuck and that he was about to lose his spectacles, which by now, were swinging from one ear. It took a while to alert fellow visitors to the Monument that something was wrong, and it took a further couple of hours until the local fire brigade had rescued him from this embarrassing position.

After nine months of hurrying every morning to the station, so that he would not miss the nine-twenty-five to Exeter, exams were looming at the Commercial College.

The results were not as successful as they might have been. In fact, the certificate for book-keeping was owed, Ronnie admitted, to the extremely kind heart of the teacher, rather than his grasp of the subject.

It would not dim his conviction that his future was bright. He was sure that his destiny was to be a writer. He had soaked up all kinds of literature; he had experienced a great number of very different educational establishments; he had met, loathed or appreciated a great variety of characters in his teachers, relatives and friends; and he himself had got entangled in several romantic relationships. By now, he felt, he was ready to earn his keep by writing, and entered confidently a commercial for a particular brand of soap. His belief in his chosen career was further strengthened when he was paid £1 for it. It went like this:

On Friday night it's Ma's delight
to bath us all at leisure
for Wright's Coal Tar, says dear old Ma,
makes bathing us a pleasure.

FIFTEEN

Success At Last and *Give Us This Day*
(1971-1972)

The critics could not be more enthusiastic about the Swann Saga and celebrate its author as 'the new Dickens':

'He is building an imposing artistic social history that promises to join those of his great forebears in the long, noble line of the English novel', writes *Life Magazine*, and not for the first time is he compared favourably with the famous: 'His narrative belongs in a tradition that goes back to John Galsworthy and Arnold Bennet.'

After his return from the USA, Ron is ready to tackle the third volume of the Swann saga, the continuation of the triumphs and disaster of the Swann family. It follows them into the times when the motor engine took over from the horse, when the troubles in Ireland began and the first signs of a World War I appeared. The Delderfield fans are impatiently awaiting its publication which is scheduled for 1973. The title will be *Give Us This Day*.

But tragedy strikes.

On the 25th June 1972, a broken-hearted May Delderfield has to tell the world that Ron has died on the previous day of lung cancer at their last residence, Dove Cottage, in Manor Road, Sidmouth.

He had been looking and feeling unwell for quite some time. His war-time friend Robert Russell met him a couple of months before at the Victory Ex-Services Club on London's Edgware Road, and thought that 'Delder was pale, slightly nervous (unheard of before) and prone to coughing.' Little did he know that Ron's condition was to prove fatal. 'I think he knew,' he adds. 'May certainly looked anguished and I left our little reunion in great disquiet.'

May explains what has happened in two very moving letters to Robert and his wife Audrey: 'At first he merely complained about tiredness, so, being friendly with our local G.P., he arranged a consultation with a specialist. He could find nothing wrong.'

Ron's publishing friend from Hodder & Stoughton, Eric McKenzie and his wife Pauline then sent him with stern words to their own private consultant in London. It was decided that Ron should have a special kind of X-ray. This showed a very small shadow outside the lung. Ron hated every minute of being prodded and dragged through hospital corridors, and when the specialist casually suggested that he would make a small incision to determine what it was, Ron just walked out and wanted to come home. He dithered for a few days, discouraged by his experience of the London hospital, but finally had the operation at Exeter Hospital.

'I was waiting for him in the hotel and we came back here,' writes May to Robert. 'This was a bad decision because the specialist in Exeter diagnosed lung cancer. I tried to persuade Ron not to have the operation because he had no lung cancer symptoms. He had this ghastly operation and they said nobody had ever shown more determination to help themselves recover. They didn't tell either of us that they had taken a section of the growth. Of course, it spread with lightning speed. It should have possibly reacted to the Cobalt Ray treatment but there they burnt his trachea with it. He went to Exeter daily for three weeks but he just became weaker. Thank goodness, he died at home, where he always was happiest amongst his books.'

In spite of his illness, Ron was determined to recover and was making plans for a trip to London to attend a Garden Party at Buckingham Palace. The booksellers Foyles had also organised one of their famous lunches for him which he did not want to miss.

May had been an enormously supportive partner in their marriage but to Ron's delight she had remained very much her own person. They had been devoted to each other, become part of each other and could not imagine life without one another.

May apologises to Robert that she would not have described Ron's illness in such detail had his old friend not asked her for it.

When Robert reminds her shortly after her husband's death, that she had actually put her own personality second, but had become just a part of Ron, she is grateful for the acknowledgement and vows to treasure his letter as a reminder how much Ron had cared for her, even though in public he did not always show his true feelings. She feels very blessed having had such a wonderful marriage.

Obituaries flood in almost immediately, even before Ron is cremated on the following Wednesday at Exeter and Devon Crematorium. Originally the service was intended as a simple family farewell, but it does not quite turn out to be that. The little chapel is filled with local friends as well as personalities from the television and book publishing world. The vicar of Sidmouth says in a short service that 'the mark of a genius has been defined as an infinite capacity to take pains. In this sense, I think, Ron Delderfield was a genius. His industry was remarkably enormous. As a result of this, he gave infinite pleasure to untold millions of people who liked his writings.'

'He will be remembered as a family man who loved his grandchildren,' he continues.

'He loved to play with them and to teach them the delights of the countryside which he loved so much, especially Devon.' He ends his sermon with the words: 'How greatly Sidmouth will miss him. How proud we have been to have had him here among us!'

On July 19th at 2.30, a memorial service is held at the request of a great number of friends, colleagues and readers, at St. Bride's in London, the church of the Fleet Street writers, arranged by Hodder & Stoughton.

During his fourteen years as a Sidmouth resident, most local people knew Ron best as the man who drove to the Esplanade in the early mornings of summer, threw off his dressing gown and enjoyed an energetic crawl around in the sea, or walking down Peak Hill or along the promenade, lost in deep conversation with local fishermen and whoever else wanted to join in.

'Ron had never any idea of time when he was with them,' May commented often.

Or people knew him as the man who came along to give an enthralling talk at the Women's Institute; or the man who occasionally wrote a protest against any move to spoil the local countryside.

A few times, he threatened to stand for council, but he ended up leaving this business to his brother Eric. Writing really did not leave him enough time for anything else.

Only his family and closest friends knew how greatly he loved music; often he would write to the background of orchestral classics.

But the vicar had been right: Most of all, Ron enjoyed meeting people and listening to them.

Ron, who had never been good with money, left to May and his children the considerable sum of £83,260 gross (or £65,862 net

136

which would have irked him immensely) according to the *Western Morning News*, but this did nothing to console his widow.

May Delderfield spent her days, until well into her eighties, at Dove Cottage where Ron had died. She enjoyed the company of family, many friends and kindly neighbours, but she did not really need looking after. Paul usually stayed with her at weekends and she enjoyed the occasional outing, accompanied by Veronica, to be interviewed about her life with the famous author.

Finally, May accepted her daughter's invitation to live with them near Exeter. There she died, surrounded by her children and grandchildren.

As if trying to make up for the delay in acknowledging his place as one of England's most popular writers, the public and the publishing world made every effort to keep his memory alive.From 1980 onwards, most of Ron's books were published in paperback, the first one being *Diana* in Coronet.

In 1978 *A Horseman Riding By* was serialised by BBC1 and broadcasted in thirteen parts. The success was astounding, only to be followed by similar acclaim in 1980 for the dramatisation of *To Serve Them All My Days*.

This unashamedly autobiographical story was shown in October 1980 on BBC1, dramatised in thirteen parts by Andrew Davies. David Powlett-Jones was played by John Duttine, Algy Herries, the eccentric headmaster, by Frank Middlemass; Beth, David's wife, was portrayed by Belinda Lang, and their two daughters Julia and Christine, by Kim Braden and Susan Jameson. Ron's old chums Boyer, Dobson, Blades, Briarley and Winterbourne all made appearances in the story and were played by Simon Gipps-Kent, Nicholas Lyndhurst, Philip Franks, Matthew Waterhouse and Grant Bardsley.

A profile of the author, with the title *Mightier Than The Sword*, was screened by the BBC in 1980 in context with the broadcasting of *To Serve Them All My Days*.

Four years later, *Diana* was shown on television and in 1983/84. Ron's erstwhile friend and colleague from Hodder & Stoughton, Eric McKenzie, was asked to set questions for the Mastermind Quiz on the topic of 'The epic novels of R.F. Delderfield', to be answered by a librarian called Jane Gardner from Swansea.

In 1984, May and her daughter Veronica were invited by Derek Robinson of the BBC to be interviewed. The woman who had devoted her life to the writer described him with shy cheekiness as 'a bit conceited but then you've got to be, haven't you, if you're a writer,' to which Veronica added: 'Daddy always knew what he wanted and he was determined to pursue it.'

'That's it,' agreed May, 'if he wasn't more gifted than the others, he was certainly more determined.'

She continued to reminisce: '*Worm's Eye View* was actually meant to be a serious play, an attack on the RAF's low pay, but humour kept breaking in. Whenever Ronnie had to get something awful off his chest, he exaggerated it enormously so that people would listen. He was always going over the top.'

She then shared another insight: 'The yardstick for his sagas was *Gone With The Wind*. I had given Ron a copy of it in 1940, which he read so many times that it had to be held together with sticky tape!'

The television series were, of course, accompanied by many articles and retrospectives into R.F. Delderfield's life. The interest in him became more intense than it had ever been while he was alive.

To this day, repeats of *A Horseman Riding By*, *Diana* and *To Serve Them All My Days* appear on various television channels and BBC Radio Four. Few people know that the first of the *Carry On* films had been written by Ron.

Over three decades after his death, Ron Delderfield is still fondly remembered by people he had come in contact with either as a friend or colleague.

John Attenborough, one-time chairman of Hodder & Stoughton, recalls in his book *A Living Memory: Hodder & Stoughton, Publishers 1868-1975*:

'...the great-hearted Ronnie Delderfield, whose untimely death deprived a huge readership of the natural successor to Howard Spring. Ronnie's habit was to write like blazes and let Robin Denniston cut the typescript down to size. That was the way of it, and the result was a succession of novels which brought the author fame right through America as well as in the British market. Success never changed him. Everybody in the firm, every bookseller he met, enjoyed the glow of his friendship. Very early in his writing career he realised that a modern publisher is more than a one-man-band. It is a team of which the author is a member.'

Their association had lasted from 1956, when the playwright was encouraged to write a sequel to *Treasure Island.*

Don Williams was another Hodder man, who had been involved in a few special promotions of Ron's books. He found him an extremely nice and helpful companion who kept everyone in high spirits with his special brand of humour. When asked about his memories of Ron, he came up, laughingly, with this remark made by the author: 'The only person who entered Parliament with the right idea was Guy Fawkes.'

Sheila Reid, wife of the late Ron Read, another Hodder employee, still remembers how much fun her late husband had, travelling round the country with Ron Delderfield and David Niven.

Eddie Bell, the Executive Chairman and Publisher of Harper Collins, agrees that 'R.F. Delderfield was an extremely professional writer.'

The West Buckland's Women's Institute staged a literary evening dedicated to R.F. Delderfield in June 1982, in the presence of his old friend 'Romeo' Boyer. This was accompanied by an exhibition of school life at West Buckland; the readings were compiled by Nigel Buckler of the Plough Theatre in Torrington and guest of honour was Frank Middlemass of the television version of *To Serve Them All My Days.*

It has gone a little quiet around the Delderfield name in the twenty-first century, but Ron's sagas are still on the shelves of major bookshops.

Veronica, his daughter, lives with her family near Exeter, being still as involved with horses as she had been when she was a little girl.

She has two sons and a daughter, Simon, who has two children himself, Edward, who married in June 1998 and Henrietta.

Paul, their uncle had withdrawn from the family's illustrious past and lead a private life somewhere around Exeter until his death in 2001.

Ron Delderfield once defined special moments in his life, which had gladdened his heart, which were near to perfect happiness, as 'butterfly-moments.' He had also believed that it was important to have a purpose in life, to identify with it, train for it and then hold fast to it.

He did just that and in the process, he brought, and still brings pleasure to his readership – 'butterfly moments' for us all.

SOURCES

Newspapers and magazines:
The Bermondsey Liberal Monthly
The Sunday Chronicle
The Sunday Express
The Sunday Telegraph
The Sunday Times
The Daily Telegraph
The Daily Mail
The Daily Sketch
The Times
The Evening Standard
Chicago Tribune
The Darlington Telegraph
The Exmouth Chronicle
Western Morning News
The Sidmouth Herald
The Express & Echo The Express & Star
The Exmouth Journal
This England
The Times Educational Supplement
The Radio Times
Devon Life
News International Newspapers Ltd.
The Literary Review
The Scotsman Publications Ltd.
Hodder & Stoughton News Sheet

Books:
Autobiographical essays by R.F. Delderfield:
Nobody Shouted Author
Bird's Eye View
Overture For Beginners
These Clicks Made History
Who's Who? 1969
Exmothiensis – School magazine of Exmouth Secondary School
West Buckland School: Tales out of School
Evans Catalogue of Acting Editions
The Guide to Selecting Plays

Smith's Trade News
Theatre World Annual
Theatre Programs:
The Playhouse
New Plays (The Ambassador Theatre)
Grand Theatre Wolverhampton (Repertory Company)
The Exmouth Players
Comedy Theatre
Grand Theatre Croydon Wimbledon Theatre Whitehall Theatre
Bexhill Theatre
Princes Theatre
St. Martin's Theatre
Teignmouth Repertory Company
Theatre World
Embassy Successes

From the West Country:
Queenie Greenaway, Exmouth
Kay Gibbens, Exmouth
Raymond Moxey, Exmouth
Mr. and Mrs. W.J. Sleeman, Exmouth
Mr. and Mrs. Geoffrey and Carol Woodhead, Honiton
Mr. Ron Hole, Buddleigh Salterton
Mr. Phillip Mussell, Exeter
Mrs. Diane Tapley, Sidmouth
Mrs. Patricia Avery, Venn Ottery
Mr. Peter Eley of 'Delderfield's' bookshop, Sidmouth
Mr. and Mrs. Ron and Sheila Reid,
Mrs. Doris M.G. Burden, Exeter
Mr. D. Brocklehurst, Sidmouth
Mr. Victor K. Robinson, Sidmouth
Mrs. Boobyer, Exmouth
Mrs. Jean Brewer of West Buckland School, Barnstaple
Mrs. Joyce Mills, Exeter
Mr. and Mrs. Steven Sylvester, Cotleigh
Mrs. Sheila Franks, Honiton
Mr. Donson of Ford, Simey,
Dow Roberts Solicitors, Exeter

RAF Friends:
Mr. Robert Russell, Wheaton Aston, Stafford
Mr. and Mrs. Bob and Dora Haken, Epsom
Mrs. Joan Plummeridge, Redhill
Mr. C.H.W. Slater, Aylesford
Mr. Derrick Robinson, Kettering
Mr. A.G. Tennant-Moon, Cheltenham
Mr. V.K. Robinson, Exmouth
Mr. Joe L. Lane, Chesterfield
Mr. Wyndham Samuel, Worthing
Mr. Jack Southwood
Mr. D. Brocklehurst, Sidmouth
Mr. Kenneth Randall, Dorchester
Mr. Grant Davidson, Grampian
Mr. L. W. Smale, Letchworth
Mr. Burt Wheeler, Horley
Mrs. Hazel Haston, Banbury
Mrs. N.K. Yeldham, Burgate Diss
Mr. Alan Thomas, AHB5 RAF
Mr. Brian Harma of the *AIRMAIL* magazine
Mr. Reg Frampton, Exmouth

Colleagues from publishing, the BBC and the theatre:
Mr. and Mrs. Eric and Pauline McKenzie, Mayfield
Mr. Robin Denniston, Great Tew
Mr. John Attenborough, Chistlehurst
Mr. Tom Salmon, Regional Television Manager BBC SouthWest
Mr. George Pridmore, Exmouth
Mr. David Spires, Producer BBC SouthWest
Mr. Ian Gibbs, Lingfield
Mr. Ken Riddington, Producer of *Diana* for the BBC
Mr. Andrew Davies, dramatisation of *Diana*
Mr. Glyn Houston, actor
Mr. John Wiles, dramatisation of *A Horseman Riding By*
Mr. and Mrs. Arden and Phoebe Winch, dramatisation of
        A Horseman Riding By
Mr. John Woodhams, Hastings
Miss Belinda Lang, actress, playing Beth in
        To Serve Them All My Days
Mr. Sermon, Bicester
Mrs. Alison Wilson, Viewer and Listener Correspondence, BBC

The following people and organisations have been helpful above duty – thank you!

Mrs. Lynette Madelin, Reference Librarian, Exeter Library
Croydon Local Studies' Library
City of London Libraries, Guildhall
Mrs. Kathleen Dickson, National Film and Television Archive
        TV Library Service
Mr. Michael Benson, Addington Palace Curator
The staff at Sevenoaks Bookshop never tired to help me in my
        research
The Book Club & Beaver Booksearch
Mrs. Linda Schofield, Marketing Manager at Pickfords
Wolverhampton Archives and Local Studies

THE FAMILY OF R.F. DELDERFIELD

Mrs. Veronica Persse, R F Delderfield's daughter
Mr. Tom Parry, married to Rita Delderfield
Mr. Robert Blake Delderfield, Benfleet
Some Delderfields who turned out to be no relation but had the
courtesy to reply

PART 2

CENTENARY ADDENDUM

CONTENTS

PREFACE

Many of you have bought and read the biography *Butterfly Moments* since its publication in December 2007. I didn't feel it was fair to ask you to buy the book again only because it had a centenary edition cover.

Hence my renewed efforts to unearth more details of R.F. Delderfield's life and work, to interview people who hadn't had a chance to come forward the first time round to tell me about their connection with him.

Next, I added all the snippets from my past research which had to be left out for various editorial reasons. As I read through it all again, I decided that I should really take a back seat in the addendum and let R.F.Delderfield speak for himself through his friends and colleagues, through his own letters and articles in which he had so passionately and eloquently explained his position on various matters.

This also allowed voices of local people to be heard who had been much closer to Ron, their friend and neighbour, than I ever had the chance to be.

I hope this will satisfy your continued curiosity about a writer who has been close to our hearts for so many years.

Some people have asked me why I hadn't started R.F. Delderfield's biography with the year of his birth and ended it with his untimely death.

To tell the truth, somewhere at the bottom of a drawer lurks a first version that did just that. Once it was finished it seemed to plod through the years of his life and lack pace and shape, rather like a pair of old bloomers' loose elastic when it should have been like a tight rubber band. It didn't seem worthy of its subject who had delighted his readership with well-crafted stories, vivid characters and a wonderful sense of humour.

Then I remembered the words of a tutor who had pressed upon us pupils that it might be more interesting to start a story at a less obvious point. Mulling this over I began to see the emergence of a chasm, the hour of a total change in my subject's life when the successful playwright Ron Delderfield had to make the dramatic decision to follow his instincts and turn into the unknown novelist R.F. Delderfield. Thank Goodness, he had the courage to face the insecurities of a new direction and could count on the support of his devoted wife May.

This watershed, I thought, would be a perfect starting point. The rest of the plot fell quite naturally into the sequence of the novels he had subsequently written: Each would remind him of a particular part of his childhood, adolescence, the years as a reporter on his father's newspaper, the RAF years and early successes as a playwright, while describing the highs and lows of his new career.

In this centenary addendum to the first edition of *Butterfly Moments*, however, I followed the natural sequence of events.

I dedicate this book to all of you who still remember R.F. Delderfield with love, affection and admiration. My hope is that our centenary celebrations and this volume will help to keep his memory alive for a good few more years and produce a new generation of R.F. Delderfield fans.

Marion Lindsey-Noble

ACKNOWLEDGEMENTS

My particular thanks for helping with this edition and the centenary celebrations go to:

Mr Richard Eley of Delderfield's, Sidmouth, who has been incredibly supportive since the first edition of my biography came out and very kindly footed the bill for my ideas to put on centenary celebrations;

Gillian Sexton who contacted me and turned into one of my staunchest supporters;

The same could be said for Jean Rees who organised the Amateur Dramatic Society of Sidmouth for me to put on a Delderfield play during the centenary year and saw to it that we got everyone together at the planning stage.

Sandria Stewart who gave up time to tell me so enthusiastically about her acting career started by her encounter with Ron who had put his trust in her acting abilities.

Mr. Peter Farmer, a busy man of the land, who willingly gave up his afternoon to speak to me and tell me about his memories of the Delderfield family.

Len Baker whose family had owned Lower Coombe Cottage and was happy to tell me about the time when the Delderfield family bought the cottage from him.

David Birch who organised for us to have Kennaway House at our disposal for the celebrations and who contacted local schools for us to instigate competitions amongst their pupils.

Mr Jamie Hodder-William who supported the celebrations from the day they were suggested, kindly donated copies of Delderfield novels for the winner's library and paid for all advertising costs.

At the time of printing, we are still hopeful that Nigel Havers and Patsy Kensit will be able to grace our celebrations which will give proceedings and everybody involved an enormous boost

Thank you all!

LONDON TO EXMOUTH

R.F. Delderfield was proud of his origins and loved his many London aunts.

His auntie Wyn still lives in Croydon where she has spent most of her life. She is over 90 years of age, a proud Quaker and with her sharp mind, lovely sense of humour and her motto 'I was lucky all my life' a great inspiration on how to grow old gracefully. She very generously spent hours to shed further light on the Delderfield's family background.

R.F. Delderfield's father William was Wyn's mother's brother.

There were eight children in that generation, all born in Bermondsey: Will, Fred, Emma, Maud, Harriet, Aida, Louise (Wyn's mother) and Nell.

Wyn's father came from a poor family and had to leave school at twelve. However, he had a quick mind, particularly for figures, and ended up in charge of a company's accounts. Uncle William, Ron's father, came often to ask his brother–in–law for financial advice

Most of the siblings have died now and the family connections still existing have loosened in old age. However, Wyn remembers that her aunt Aida married a widower and had two daughters.

Aunt Maud's story was rather tragic: Her husband was transferred to South Africa and died there from tuberculosis within six months. Maud and her two daughters, called Olive and Ivy, had to return to England, where they lived with the grandparents and Maud found employment as a matron. Ivy died at the age of twenty while Olive was still alive at the writing of this book.

Wyn's auntie Nell married George who died when their boys were three years old. They were close to Uncle Will, Ron's father, who visited them frequently in Catford where they lived. Even after her husband's death, auntie Nell stayed always close to Ron's family.

Wyn remembers her uncle William well who hated swearing but used the word 'faktet' when he got upset. Nobody knew where it derived from but it was assumed that it meant 'fathead'. His wife, Wyn's auntie Alice was nice, prim and proper and keen that her boys should behave themselves.

During the First World War, Wyn's father moved the family to Ashburton Avenue where they lived in no.14. Soon afterwards,

Ron's family followed to escape the bombings of London and settled into no.22, only five minutes walk from the ruins of the old military academy set up by the East India Company.

Wyn was five and Ron thirteen, when they all lived in Addiscombe. She remembers that everyone went to Selhurst Grammar School where the Delderfield boys were always in trouble. Ron, it was said, had knocked the headmistress off her bicycle and at another occasion he had climbed out of the window. One of the teachers in his desperation had warned Ron: 'You will never get anywhere, Delderfield'.

Uncle Will was meant to punish the boys on his return in the evenings, but to the disappointment of his wife, he never did.

If the truth be known, Uncle Will would probably have stayed in the capital as most of his sisters had stayed in the square mile of Tower Bridge. However, considering his wife's fragile state of mind, it was better for the family to move to the quieter suburb. To compensate, Ron's father developed the habit of disappearing at regular intervals for three or four days for reunions or to simply walk the streets of his beloved London.

Ron may have been a tearaway but he had other qualities – he loved reading, became fond of history and, having only known inner city life, loved to roam in his new surroundings; to him it was the countryside and he couldn't have been more taken with it. Wyn recognised Manor Hill when reading The Avenue Saga years later.

Then one day, her cousin's family suddenly moved from Addiscombe to Exmouth in Devon. The next time Wyn met him was when her family was invited to spend a holiday in East Devon.

The abiding memory of that trip was that Ron and Eric had dug a big hole in the sand with steps leading down into it. They then asked little Wyn to try it out and Ron got very cross when she broke the steps in the process. The fathers insisted that the boys fill in the hole as it was dangerous.

After that Wyn didn't see Ron until 1937, when she stayed with Eric, his brother, and Dora, Eric's wife, who had a daughter called June.

Ron did all the talking, light-heartedly and full of fun. May prodded him occasionally when he became over- enthusiastic.

Ron had been best man at his brother's wedding to Dora, and Wyn had been a bridesmaid.

According to her, Eric was blustering; the brothers were politically miles apart and had frequent feuds. Family gossip, as always to be taken with a pinch of salt, reported that May had first gone out with Eric, maybe just wishful thinking on Eric's part after they had both met May on a holiday in Wales and she had to return to Manchester at the end of it.

Dora was killed in a car crash and Eric's second marriage was a disaster. They got divorced and when Wyn met him next he lived with a very nice woman and her daughter Jenny.

Wyn didn't endear herself with Eric when she said: 'I didn't know you wrote as well.'

Wyn has never met Veronica, Ron and May's daughter, but she had heard that Ron had burst out laughing when she introduced her fiancé: he was a soldier and Ron and May were both anti-war.

The London relatives were proud of Ron's achievements and whenever there was a performance of one of his plays all the family went to the theatre in Hammersmith or to the Whitehall in London to see *Worm's Eye View*.

During the Second World War, Wyn's family were evacuated to Buckinghamshire. Ron must have visited them there and called in because he inscribed a volume of *Nobody Shouted Author* with the words: Remembering your kindness 1942-1944, given to them in September 1957

In 1963, they visited Ron and May again who took them to an auction. They met at the shop where Ron and Eric were having a flaming row. Ron laughed saying: 'This is the way we start the morning!'

I am really grateful to Wyn that she let me have those wedding photographs, precious mementos which I returned as soon as I had made copies.

****

There are still a few people in Exmouth, Devon, who remember or have heard from older relatives of the arrival of the Delderfields. Their father had no previous experience with newspapers, but set about taking over the *Exmouth Chronicle* with great enthusiasm and zeal. He was a sociable man and soon well known and respected while his wife Alice positively bloomed being in charge of the shop adjacent to the printing works.

Young Ron and his good pal Cyril were often the cause of much hand-wringing and shaking of heads. David Lee was Cyril's nephew. His mother Doreen Chown had owned the motorbike which Cyril drove without permission when he famously lost his pillion passenger Ron in the process.

David's grandfather was the Sunday school Superintendent of the Glenorchy Congregational Church where the assegai incident took place in the large schoolroom.

David kindly confirmed that Thirza Parsons was the old family retainer who worked for the family on and off for about 60 years. When he and his sister were small, Thirza used to come one night a week to bath them and told the tales of Ron and Cyril's escapades. The incident of pillows being emptied over passers-by to make it snow, David corrected me, did not happen at Ron's house but at David's grand-parents' home at 14 Rolle Street. However, Thirza did give in her notice as a result, as she had done so several times before.

Cyril died in February 1973 of lung cancer as his friend Ron had succumbed to the same illness almost a year earlier.

Ron's time at The Grange in Class 3 B was a happy one from the point of view that he could continue to be the lad until the 'Brickyard Scandal' put an end to it. The late Kay Gibbons shed a little more light on it which seemed to have been due to one girl's escapades: Muriel Shearing. According to Kay 'everyone called her Cis. She had three sisters: Rose, Helen and Myrtle. Cis had a fatal fascination for the boys and was somewhat envied by all us girls! She married Don Gibson and they emigrated to Australia.'

Holidays were spent camping with his pals Arthur Islip and Ken Coombes on the top of the cliffs at Sandy Bay to where they invited other friends like Kay Gibbons, Bob Gough and Jack Southwood. They also went along on Sunday's when Ron was made to attend the religious meetings at the Y.M.C.A. Hall called The Brotherhood, to support him. As Kay Gibbons once described it: 'The meetings were more of a source of amusement than religious content owing to the vociferous addresses of Messrs Delderfield and Chown!'

Once Ron had left West Buckland School, he formed a concert party with his friends, playing the Ukelele and singing funny duets with Ken Coombes, while Kay sang and played the piano. The group was always very warmly welcomed in the neighbouring villages of Woodbury, Otterton and East Budleigh.

On one occasion, Ron organised a concert at the Pavilion in Exmouth in aid of the Carnival funds, which was packed to the doors

After his marriage to May, Kay often visited the couple in Oak

Park, Bradbourne Lane. Kay went on to produce many plays and be the shining light at the Blackmore Theatre in Exmouth. Many people expected her and Ron to get married, but she just laughed it off, saying that she had been the only girl who hadn't resented Ron marrying May. 'I was far too outgoing and not demure enough. May was perfect for him!'.

He was very disappointed when his play *Spark in Judea* failed to be made into a film with Basil Rathbone in the lead part, but The Exmouth Players produced *Worm's Eye View* (the second time by Kay) and subsequently put on *The Queen Came By* and *Once Aboard the Lugger* which were roaring successes.

To Ron, Exmouth was nothing like the Addiscombe suburb; one became an Exmothian; provincialism reigned. Half-hearted in its attempts at attracting visitors, it was however strong on amateur dramatics which suited him fine. Ron lived with his parents in Salterton Road round the corner from Kenneth E. Rendall. When Mr. Rendall fell ill, Ron came round with great regularity to bring him books for entertainment.

Jack Southwood replied years ago in his tiny, neat handwriting from Ryll Grove, not far from where Ron's brother Eric lived, telling me about the constant battles Ron had with teachers, particularly a man called Harry who was teaching woodwork and PE for which he wasn't really qualified. Most of the PE lessons were outside as the school didn't have a gym before 1926. Harry had a hard time to cope with the argumentative young Delderfield and often suffered under his inventive experiments in woodwork which had not been on the lesson plan.

One day, Harry thought he might get his own back. The PE lesson was cancelled due to pouring rain and replaced by a session of woodwork introducing the class to various types of wood, in particular conifers. Mentioning that some of the cones might reach a length of eight inches, the teacher was soon embroiled in an argument with Ron who insisted that he had seen much longer ones in the school grounds. Exasperated, Ron was sent out into the pouring rain to fetch such a specimen. Suffice to say that Ron did return, soaking wet, with the eight foot branch of a monkey puzzle tree which had crowned the drive up to the school.

West Buckland School could cope much better with that sort of unstoppable spirit. Ron felt a great attachment to the school and in later years tried to attend the reunions every Whitsun. In a way he had enjoyed the gratuitous popularity if not to say notoriety to play the buffoon, tending to dramatise everyday situations. He was not embarrassed about his cockney accent which he preserved to the end of his life. This atmosphere of affectionate tolerance of a sometimes wayward boy made Ron into a stout champion of teenagers. He had appreciated being supported and believed in when others had despaired of him.

There were times later on, when he regretted not having made more effort at school and realised that without significant qualifications and in view of high unemployment in the West Country he had limited himself to working on his father's newspaper, but like so many people, he found a way out, first as a playwright and later on as a novelist. It was a time of frustration and claustrophobia in being tied to one place, but it had also its benefits which he very quickly realised and hung on to. Journalism taught him one thing in particular: That there is at least one good story in everyone, and never to neglect the most insignificant news item. Hence his wife's comment when asked where her husband was most likely to be: 'He'll be down by the harbour, chatting to fishermen.' Showing interest in everybody and in what they had to say was one of Ron's most endearing traits. Many of these chats and characters found their way into his plays and stories.

Politically, Ron had always been a Liberal, but after reading Koestler's Spanish Testament his mind made a somersault and from advocating disarmament, Ron wrote leading articles urging for re-armament. His conservative friends thought he had gone weak in the head. When Edward VIII abdicated not even the scores of retired admirals and major-generals of Budleigh Salterton had an inkling of what was to come. Edward had been liked for his vitality and informality and Ron got annoyed at this sudden outburst of puritanical rectitude amongst the citizens, calling it a Domestic Crisis. As he once wrote: 'For a week, the British public danced on the corpse and then, feeling rather foolish, they returned to their cricket and their crumpets beside the fire and promptly forgot all about him.'

While working at the *Exmouth Chronicle*, Ron met Clem Attlee at a small private tea party, when he came to the West to rally the cause of Labour. Ron managed to have thirty minutes with him without other pressmen being there. Attlee was thought rather dull, but Ron was impressed and found him to be 'the very best type of Englishman, compassionate, working for the underprivileged, with Christian ethics but the good manners not to wave them like banners'.

By 1938 few people had been frank about their reaction to Munich: Ron shared the general relief when Chamberlain stepped down from that plane, smiling his rabbit-toothed smile, and waving his famous piece of paper, but nobody was reassured and not long afterwards he resigned himself to Armageddon.

Worm's Eye View was an accumulation of ideas and experiences from spring 1940 to winter 1943. Ron wanted to capture the sense of oneness with a million unidentified men and a sense of kinship: 'No amount of post-war disillusionment can touch or tarnish my love and respect for the ordinary British man and girl... And of course, the comedy of it all!'

THE GAZEBO
PEAK HILL
SIDMOUTH.
DEVON
PHONE SIDMOUTH 3308

July 22. '61

Dear Mr Delderfield.

Many thanks for your second letter & enclosures. I was particularly struck by the possibility. We had a Rector in the family!! I enclose two photos – the larger is my great-grandfather, (presumably the W.J. aged 5 on your chart), the smaller my grandfather & grandmother. I imagine our common great-great grandfather was Joseph the Tanner, born 1801. Does this tie up with your deductions?

Sincerely.

R.F. Delderfield

Please let me have the pictures back!

Aug 17. 69

Dear Mr D.

In haste — as ever!

Many thanks for tracing the romance of Becky & Bill in Wright's Buildings! He seems to have been outrageously hemmed in by in-laws & was obviously a precocious 15! Well in the family tradition!

When I get through with the 700-page proofs of the new saga I'll make out a chart of all the Dellenfields I know on our side & send it on, for your comments & corrections.

Have you got hold of 'For My Own Amusement' yet? A lot of them are in there.

As Ever.

Ronnie D.

160

May 21. 70

My Dear Bob. I am sorry I took so long to thank you for all the hard work you did on behalf of the ancestors & for being so kind as to work out the tree for me. I have been snowed under with a 3000 mile tour to promote 'God Is An Englishman' Vol I of the Swann Saga, finishing the sequel, Vol II (due out next year) & supervising the production of a comedy premiere here in Sidmouth. My corres. has lagged.

Many congratulations on Lynn. I love that name & I will make one of Swann's granddaughters a Lynn. It seems that the Digger Branch of the Delderfields continues to expand. My brother Bill has three grandchildren & the eldest has just married. Every time I get a Delderfield-relation claim I automatically shuttle them on

continued overleaf

161

to you. I hope you approve of this
as — of all the clan — you must
surely qualify as its archivist.

My father told me grandfather
W.J. has a 'K' leg — caused
through carrying skins up flights
of stairs at the Bermondsey
tannery. This seems to tie-in
with his nickname.

There can be no doubt, I think,
but that we are all originally
Huguenot stock. We all seem to
originate from the south-east where
the exiles settled, late 17th
century, follows the 'revocation of
the Edict of Nantes. All seem to
be craftsmen. In myself I have
a 50/50 strain — Celt & Frank. The
former supplies creative imagination,
the latter Norman 'organisation' of
material — a happy coincidence
in a professional writer who
has to <u>sell</u> as well as invent.

My warmest regards.
Very Sincerely.
Ronnie D

162

Sept 2nd '70

My Dear Bob. I have just returned from
planting the Deddington banner in
N. York & Chicago & am swamped. 'God
Is An Englishman' is a best-seller
there — hence the lachsity & brevity
of this note.

Many thanks for most
interesting & amusing notes that I
am sending on to my elder brother Bill
in Tasmania. My son Paul is with him —
we do get around!

I am sending you an
inscribed book as soon as I get
around to wrapping it. Note
change of address.

As Ever,

Ronnie

163

R.F. Delderfield at his brother's weddding

THE RAF YEARS

One of R.F. Delderfield's most enduring friendships from the RAF was with Robert Russell. Before his death he wrote reams of his war time memories – in particular about their time together at Hinton-in-the-Hedges. It had been one of those 'Hide and Seek' camps, forgotten groups of men who enjoyed a lot of freedom, until someone in high places remembered them and sent them abroad.

Robert's stories still make me laugh. He admired Ron not only for his story-telling but even more so for his talents in organising the cooks who seemed to be absent every other day thanks to the administrative shenanigans of their pal Delder in the Orderly Room Central Registry; in return the company was woken daily at 6.30 am with hot tea, Libby's milk and a mug of sugar, followed at 7 am by bacon butties.

The daily run in a Dennis flat-topped lorry, which was sent to collect and deliver urgent aircraft replacement parts from the Railway Station at Brackley, a mile or so away, was often diverted by 'Delder' and his friends under the pretext that they had to check 'movement orders'. The pick up took no time at all, after which Dennis, the driver, parked the lorry by Brackley Town Hall just opposite a small tea shop. There they could be found scoffing home baked scones and drinking coffee in exchange for some RAF delicacy like a pound of lard, while discussing 'Delder's' play *Printer's Devil* which they wanted to put on stage at their RAF Station.

'Delder', a willing and patriotic RAF man, but not gritty soldier material, sometimes left his friends to pick hot potatoes out of the fire for him: LACW Joan Pugsley, otherwise known as 'Deep Bosomed Joan', begged Robert to return a call on behalf of the absent Ron to his mighty agent Margery Vosper. Where was her client? Ron had gone on leave to Exmouth without having replied to any of her messages or letting her know his whereabouts. The whole company was listening in to that rather flustered conversation between Robert who was totally out of his depth and the forceful Miss Voster.

The two letters printed below give an insight into Ron's life as an author of novels while at the same time allowing a glimpse of the friendships of his RAF years. Dora Haken had treasured those letters for years. By the time I met her, she was ill with cancer, but had made an enormous effort to refuse my offer of coming to see her and came to find me in my Kent cottage; even then she still looked 'quite the prettiest, elegant lady'. I am not surprised Ron remembered her immediately when he received her letters. He would have liked her husband, too, an English gentleman of the old school, dapper, with a moustache and laughter lines around the eyes, and very protective of his fragile but determined wife.

The Gazebo.

Oct. 11. 67.

My Dear Dora,
In haste. Many thanks for the photo — you don't look like a casualty! I enclose a note for you to take to the manager at Smith's who will remember me. If you don't get any satisfaction cross the road to the well-known bookshop opposite. If — after all this — you ever actually own a book by me I enclose a sticker to give it a personal note.

As Ever.
Ron.

The bearer is an old friend of mine who was in the R.A.F. & is very keen to get a copy of 'On the Fiddle', the Hodder paperback. I would be grateful if you got her one as soon as possible. Did you see the write-up in the 'Advertiser'?

Greetings.

R.F. Delderfield

Dear Mr Deniston,

Re attached. I was the R.A.F. officer attached to Staff who covered the Balloon Barrage defence of the V bomb attack, and was also the first Englishman to report on their sites, which I covered extensively in the autumn of '44. I was also the man who interviewed many of the FFI spies who sent us the 'gen'. If you would like me to review this book in any way, or give it a boost quote, I'd be glad to.

Ronnie D

An undated letter written to his publisher from Peak Cottage referring to his time in the RAF.

The Gazebo.
~~PEAK COTTAGE~~
PEAK HILL
SIDMOUTH
DEVON
PHONE SIDMOUTH 3308

Sept. 20. '67.

My Dear Dora,

How pleasant to get a
letter from you after all these years. (I
had one previously, when you lived in
Croydon but not, I believe, in Addington) &
now you must be near the exact spot
where I saw my first primrose in 1918!
It was in the woods on the left of Sprout
Hill & the country between Shirley Rd &
Cudham was a wilderness of farms &
lanes & coppices! Where are they all now?

I remember you equally well —
you were quite the prettiest waif at
Hinton — & the play we did was 'Printer's
Devil', later to appear on the West End
& films as 'All Over the Town'. It is
a paperback too, but the paperback you
would enjoy (for you would recognise Hinton)
is 'On the Fiddle', where I parodied
every camp I ever served on. It was
Shaun Connery's first film in which he

played a leading role. The booklet you saw in Cornwall is my brother who does Guidebooks etc & the similarity in initials is a damned nuisance.

I don't write for the stage much now, although a play of mine on Victoria will appear at the Yvonne Arnaud Theatre soon, in Guildford, — keep your eye open for it. I either do long family sagas like 'Horseman' or biographical studies on Napoleon, here & in U.S.A. If you enjoyed the plays I think you might like the novel, 'Horseman'. The sequel comes out in May.

Our two children are now 23 & 21! The girl, Veronica, is married to a helicopter pilot in the R.M. in Singapore & has one boy, the boy is on a farriers course at Hereford.

If you ever get hold of a book of mine I'd like to write something in it as a memento of that crazy camp, & I'll certainly ring you up if I'm ever in the Croydon area.

All the very best & happy memories of Hinton.

Ron

169

EXMOUTH, SIDMOUTH AND THE PLAYWRIGHT

Ron loved to write plays, was enormously successful with one of them, *Worm's Eye View*, but could never repeat that sort of nationwide success in spite of churning them out tirelessly.

Exmouth and Sidmouth Amateur Dramatic Societies both benefitted from R.F. Delderfield living amongst them because they were often asked to try out the plays on local audiences before they would be offered to a London theatre, provincial stage or the BBC to turn them into radio plays.

Interviewed after the premier of his play *Once Aboard the Lugger* staged by the Exmouth Players in 1962 at the Pavilion in Exmouth (produced by Oswald Bussell), Ron gave his honest opinion on plays of that time: 'I wrote this to make a pleasant evening, because so many of the present playwriters seem to be so sorry for themselves.' He wanted to entertain and make people laugh!

However lukewarm the national response might have been, his fellow citizens loyally supported his efforts and had enormous fun in the process; so much so that forty years after the author's death, the towns' thespians jumped at the chance to pay their particular kind of homage on the occasion of his 100th birthday.

Sandria Stewart or Pickard, as she was known then, will be forever grateful to Ron giving her the chance to be in one of his plays, *The Key of the Hut* at the Manor Pavilion, directed by the famous Gene Gerrard who in retirement had moved down to East Devon. Sandria had such a wonderful time playing the role of Margy and discovered how much she enjoyed acting that it set her on the path of a career in the theatres: 'It will be forty years this June,' she said wistfully when I met her in 2010.

She remembers Ron as quite flirtatious, May as very nice, but a little shy, meeting her sometimes at local auctions. Sandria still treasures a programme signed by Ron with the words: 'You can blackmail me any time!' referring to her role in the play.

When the Exmouth Chronicle at which Ron had been a reporter was sold, he set about writing furiously – every day from 9 to 5 with an hour lunch break. He felt lonely, neither belonging to the newspaper world any more nor feeling at home in the theatre world. He ended up with violent headaches and was prescribed fresh air and horse riding.

By 1956 at the age of almost forty-four, Ron had struggled enough for recognition and a repeat of the success of *Worm's Eye View*. It wasn't to be, he had a family to look after, he had to try something else, and anyway, he yearned to write novels, long stories about people and places from his past. On the first of January that year he gave himself permission to do so.

Theatre Productions:

THE KEY OF THE HUT
Performed by Sidmouth Dramatic Society, May 1970

Ethel Buck	JILLIAN POWELL
Vernon Ironmaster	PHILIP DWERRYHOUSE
Elizabeth	WENDY HAY
Oswald Manning	TIM SEATON
Margy	SANDRIA PICKARD
Hubert Sutcliffe-Manning	SYDNEY ANDREW
Maybelle Manning, J.P	BARBARA TOWELL
George	DAVID POOL
Mrs. Mallowfield	NELL LIBBIS

PEACE COMES TO PECKHAM
Princes Theatre, London

Characters in order of their appearance:

George Palfrey	LESLIE DWYER
Nurse Ironside	BERTHA BELMORE
'Erbie Gilpin	PETER SCOTT
Frank Gilpin	JOHN WYNN
Grace Palfrey	MYRTLE REED
Alice Palfrey (Lal.)	ELLA RETFORD
Dr. Bramley	ALFRED HARRIS
Harry Palfrey	LIONEL BLAIR
Gloria Palfrey	DIANA DECKER
Zebedee	A. PARROT
Huck Kauffman	JEFFERSON SEARLES

Directed by Anthony Hawtrey and Wallace Douglas

WHERE THERE'S A WILL

Presented at the "Q" Theatre under the title *Follow the Plough* in 1953
with the following cast of characters:

"Cagey" Narracott, handyman at Windrush Farm	JAN STEWER
Lawyer Arscott	CHRISTOPHER STEELE
Annie Yeo, housekeeper at Windrush Farm	MARJORIE RHODES
"Mafeking" Brewer	FREDERICK PEISLEY
Alfie Brewer	LESLIE DWYER
Amy Slater, his younger sister	DORIS YORKE
Maud Hodge, his elder sister	DANDY NICHOLS
Fred Slater, his brother-in-law	GORDON BELL
June Hodge, Maud's daughter	DILYS LAY
Ralph Stokes	GLYN HOUSTON
Miss Cogent	GWEN NELSON

Directed by Chloe Gibson

Subsequently produced by Jack Paye and Will Hammer at the Garrick
Theatre, London, in 1954 with the following cast of characters:

"Cagey" Narracott	SIDNEY MONCKTON
Lawyer Arscott	DEREK TANSLEY
Annie Yeo	MARJORIE RHODES
"Mafeking" Brewer	ERIK CHITTY
Alfie Brewer	LESLIE DWYER
Amy Slater	DORIS YORKE
Maud Hodge	BETTY WARREN
Fred Slater	BILL OWEN
June Hodge	PAT SANDYS
Ralph Stokes	EDWARD WOODWARD
Mr Cogent	CHARLES LEPPER

Directed by Frank Shelley

THE ORCHARD WALLS

Characters in order of their appearance

Rachel Ames	MAUREEN O'REILLY
Philip O'Hea	CYRIL RAYMOND
Beatrice Maynard	GILLIAN LIND
Christine Muir	VALERIE WHITE
Michael Pritchard	JOHN CHARLESWORTH
Nicholas Stubbs	COLIN DOUGLAS
Mrs. Grant	HELEN HORSEY
Godfrey Pritchard	EDWARD EVANS
Shirley Grant	DOROTHY GORDON

Directed by John Forbes-Sempill

WAGGONLOAD O' MONKEYS
Performed by Teignmouth Repertory company

Willie Dawn	S.S DOWSING
Evie Dawn	MURIEL GARDINE
'Scrumpy' Tapscott	ERIC VOSPER
Percy Hetherington-Gore	NIGEL POTTAGE
Sam Porter	PETER K. PEARCE
Taffy	COLIN RICHARDS
Thelma	TRUDI IVESON
Philip Johnson	ROBBIE WEEKES
Mr. Bancroft	GRENVILLE GOULD

Produced by Sydney Homewood

WORM'S EYE VIEW

Performed by West Buckland School and reviewed in the school magazine by Ron Delderfield:

"Producer H.A. Boyer ("Romeo" to me), who was virtually responsible for presenting *Worm's Eye View* on the West Buckland stage last term, has asked me, as author and his contemporary at West Buckland, to write my impressions of the play for the Register. I do so gladly, partly because, when at School, I attained to such distinction (1 mean writing it the Register) and partly because I have seldom enjoyed an evening so much. That goes for my wile too. Both of us have yawned our way through the play countless times. We know every move, every cough… but this time, it was different.

"Just how different I find it difficult to say. Although I have seen the play done by amateurs, professionals, and rep. companies, I have never before seen every role played by a male and the situations, plus the audience's reactions to those situations, were so fresh and unexpected that I might have been watching a new play.

"Let me say to start with that the production was a great credit to Mr. Boyer, his cast and his stage team. The pace was spanking and the lively appreciation of minor quips on the part of the audience was a sure indication that the billetees were determined to extract every laugh from every scene and then some!

"To me the play had a freshness and vitality that it has lacked on some previous occasions. The stage management was slick and unobtrusive and this contributed in large measure to the maintenance of pace throughout the three acts. On the night I saw it, the play never flagged for a second. Another interesting feature of this show was the team-work of the cast. Honours were shared, and nobody tried to get away with anyone else's lines.

"I particularly praised N.D. Pratt's work as Belle, when I spoke from the stage, because his task was that much harder than the others. He had to play against laughter the whole time and it staggered me to see that not once did he get; a gratuitous laugh on account of his sex. His sense of the theatre is a real one. J.F. Nicholson, as the landlady. has a very obvious comic gift and would have been a success anywhere in that role. T. Bradford, as Thelma, also played with plenty of sparkle and I particularly commend her for her resource when she dropped the parcel and retrieved it without breaking the continuity of the scene. I doubt whether many professionals could have done that as deftly as she did.

"It was a joy to see C.L. Dunn as my favourite character, Pop. Somehow, to me, he was Pop. He understood every line of the part and played it gently, quietly, and sincerely.

"It did not occur to me until J.B. Dobson (Corporal Mark) said that line "It was a small public school in North Devon..." that I had West Buckland in mind when I wrote his part away back in 1944. Dobson played with forcefulness and charm and his love scene in Act Two was brilliantly done.

"Porter (played by G.E. Hern) did not dominate the play 11 as he does in some productions. He was just "one of the boys and the sharpest of them. Because of this I liked his performance. He saved something for Act Three and did not fire all his ammo. in the preceding acts. F.R. Bowen, as the possessor of the only true Welsh accent ill the School, was a "natural" as Taffy and a good feed to his partner. J.H. Armstrong, as the philandering Duke, rounded off a confident and extremely lively quintet of airmen. I have seldom heard amateurs more word-perfect. They did not take a single prompt.

"H.V. Pike made the most of the exacting and unsympathetic part of Sydney Spooner. J.B. Richards also had a difficult. role in Mr. Bounty, playing several tunes his age. He did it very well, and in addition, made sound work of the Lancashire accent. W.F. Dale, as S/Ldr. Briarly, brought the house down with his moustache and it is to his credit that he could play against such a wall of laughter.

"Well Romeo, mon vieux, you did a grand job and it was a real joy to watch. I hope these notes are seen by Messrs. Boyce, Grant, Cooper, Beer, Bellew, Pedder, and Gluning, the stage-team without whom the cast's efforts – no matter how good – would have been wasted.

"I was very touched by the wonderful ovation the school gave me and as I said at the time – it was wonderful to be able to go backstage and to mean everything one said about a production!

Gratefully,
R.F.D."

SIDMOUTH, BUDLEIGH SALTERTON
AND THE NOVELIST

Ron had felt blessed to live in one of the most beautiful parts of our country: 'unspoilt countryside where nobody carries umbrellas or catches regular trains.'

He made friends where ever he went not because he was the famous playwright, prolific journalist or well-known novelist but because he was a lovely man. All his life, he had remained the London Cockney who had fallen in love with the West Country and its people, passionately interested in everybody's lives, woes and opinions.

Even people who haven't met him can feel an affinity through his books. A Mr.Tuff rang me from Stockport in Cheshire to say that he had been born on the day R.F. Delderfield had died, that the 371 bus from near his house goes straight to the village where May Delderfield used to live and that since reading the novels he had visited Exmouth twice yearly with a particular link to the town's museum. I know it may sound far fetched but what I could hear between the lines of these coincidences was the desire that the man would have dearly loved to meet Ron. It was the effect Ron had on people which I had encountered many times during my research.

Mrs. Annette Brown rang up to say that she remembered Mr. Delderfield when he was walking with his black Labrador along the promenade in the mornings. He was always wearing a polo neck jumper. Mrs. Brown was then 16 years old and working at Mr. Govier's gift shop opposite the beach in Sidmouth to earn money to go to college. On the few occasions that she had an opportunity to speak to him she found him lovely, approachable without 'airs and graces'.

Councillor Sylvia Carr and her husband were so very kind to write down their memories of Ron Delderfield and send them via the town clerk, Trina Jarrett. Mr. and Mrs. Carr have been Sidmouth residents all their lives and of course, came in contact with the author.

Mr. Carr was a milkman and remembers vividly knocking on the door of the Gazebo and most times to his surprise, it was the famous man himself opening it and settling the monthly milk account; but then, Mr. Carr explains, it was the 'acute observations of the mundane, the simple day to day events and doings of ordinary folk that lent such charm and realism to his many literary successes.' Mr.

Carr ends his letter by saying that 'Ronald Frederick Delderfield was a unique character and I count myself privileged to have met him – however briefly.'

Mrs. Carr had never spoken to Ron, but had seen him walking around Sidmouth. She had always loved his books and when in later years, she met May and told her about it, 'Mrs. Delderfield smiled and expressed her thanks that someone would still remember him.'

Gillian Sexton from Tipton St. John was very proud to be connected in a rather special way to the Delderfields. She took enormous trouble to unearth pages of manuscripts and other memorabilia of the time when her late mother had been Ron's PA/secretary (1968 – 1972). His previous aide, Miss Stern, had retired and recommended her successor. Gillian remembers her mother's employer as a big man with a big, blue Mercedes who was so nice, patient, cheerful and generous. He gave them copies of the books Helen had typed inscribed with words of gratitude, and a large, original painting which was the cover for one of the books' American version.

Gillian Sexton lives now almost next door to Lower Coombe Cottage where Ron and May had resided when *A Horseman Riding By* was in progress. It is the proverbial picture postcard or chocolate box cottage with a thatched roof, steps down into the kitchen and an old-fashioned cottage garden.

Mr. Len Baker had sold it to the Delderfield's for £710 in 1957. Ron had a bungalow built in the orchard for Mrs. Evans, May's mother, who had joined them from Manchester.

The previous cellar was turned into a kitchen, an Aga was installed but demanded alterations to the chimney and kitchen floor.. A window was put in the upstairs bathroom and the cottage was connected to the sewage and mains water systems. It was painted pink for the Delderfields and a white picket fence erected around the property. Mr. Baker also built a study in the garden for Ron to write in.

Len remembers Ron as big in stature, about 6'2" to his own 5'9" with Ronny Barker glasses and a loud Cockney voice sounding like Michael Caine. He would tell him that he had bought the cottage with money brought in by Ron Shiner's film. Len is convinced that Lower Coombe Cottage features in *A Horseman Riding By*, but that there are no such splendid views in reality as described in the book.

Len helped the family move into Lower Coombe Cottage and as always, Ron was hopelessly generous with money and paid two shillings and sixpence for a twenty minute job which was in those days two hours' wages.

Len still remembers fondly how he was given a ride in the pale-blue Daimler Sovereign feeling like a lord in the back seat.

My visit at Gillian Sexton's home led to an introduction to Mr. Pete Farmer at Higher Coombe Farm, a couple of minutes walk up the hill.

In spite of a busy farming schedule, he took the time to tell me about his connection with the Delderfields. He got to know the family very well because he had befriended their son Paul who was a bit of a loner. He introduced him to country pursuits like rabbiting, ferreting and shooting starlings. Paul had been a day boy in one of the posh schools, but preferred roaming the countryside with his new pal.

Pete was frequently taken along on Delderfield family outings as company for Paul. He remembers particularly a beautiful day in the Doone Valley on Exmoor and recalls how petrified he was being taken to a posh restaurant, desperate to mind his manners and not to embarrass himself and his hosts.

The teenage Pete thought Veronica who was by then around 17 years of age, a very attractive young lady who, it was rumoured, was impressed by men in uniforms; well, as we all know, she married a Royal Marine Officer, no less, Mr.Richard Persse.

Ron often turned up at Higher Coombe Farm to buy eggs when the Farmers had just started dinner. Nobody minded because he was very entertaining, chatting nineteen to a dozen; in fact Mr. Farmer appreciated the company after a day alone out in the field. As the Farmer family were Conservatives and Ron a Liberal there was an awful lot to discuss and argue over.

After about four years, the Delderfields moved on and Pete lost contact with them. He met Paul briefly in Sidmouth when he was about twenty-seven and later on, Ron who seeing that Pete had just bought an engagement ring for his Swedish fiancée, congratulated him 'on his excellent taste in women'.

Now to something totally different…

Please, indulge me.

Have you ever wondered whether there was a house which had impressed Ron so much that he put it at the heart of a novel?

Remember Adam and Henrietta Swann's grand house in *God Is An Englishman* 'squatting between the two dark spurs of woodland… looking like a self-indulgent old man'?

I found it! Funnily enough, I had been driving past its gates every day of my working week for seventeen years. I lived in a village in Kent, was teaching at a school in Shirley near Croydon (and Addiscombe!) and, to avoid the traffic, took the country roads via Spout Hill.

Croydon Library helped me in my research and managed to shed more light on the matter. I ended up with an invitation to the mansion which was first called Addington Park and later on Addington Palace. The present owners who had turned it into a posh country club cared enough about it to employ a curator who told me all about its history:

There had been a castle on this site since the thirteenth century which at some stage burnt down. In 1447, the Estate was purchased by the Leigh family for £38,500 who sold it in 1768 to Barlow Trecothick, a self-made city merchant and the then Lord Mayor of London. It was rumoured that he had made his fortune in the North American trade. In 1772, he built the present house and in 1780/1, employed Capability Brown to landscape the huge grounds.

However, only two years later, everything was put up for auction but failed to attract immediate interest. Finally, in 1808 it became, by an Act of Parliament, the suburban residence of six successive Archbishops of Canterbury (one of whom crowned Queen Victoria) – hence the name change to Addington Palace. Duly, a little chapel was built in the 1840s, and a fine library and more bedrooms added. It was also said that an exceptionally fine Cedar of Lebanon was planted and a beautiful avenue of elms created which lead to the little church which is supposed to have stood on the site of a hunting lodge belonging to Henry VIII. In all, the mansion had 45 bedrooms, a dozen bathrooms and 12,000 acres of ground.

In 1896, Archbishop Temple decided to live at Canterbury, and Addington Palace was bought by Frederick Alexander English, a millionaire diamond dealer from South Africa. He spent £70,000 on its refurbishment. After Mr. English's death, the estate was again put to auction but found no takers.

Between 1914 and 1918, Addington Palace was used as a war hospital, 1928-51 as a golf and country club (to which it had reverted when I visited) and was finally purchased in 1951 by the Croydon Corporation for £47,500 – who let it to the The Royal School of Church Music; this was opened in July 1954 by H.M. Queen Elizabeth the Queen Mother.

I have no idea whether Ron knew about the history of the original

'Tryst' – given his interest in history he might well have made enquiries – but I am sure he would have been as impressed as I had been walking down the elm-lined avenue back to my car.

Addington Place, the Seat of James Trecothick Esq.
Published as the Act directs by RBaldwin Nov.r 1st 1782.

An engraving of Addington Place published in 1782

FREEHOLD MANOR, PERPETUAL ADVOWSON, GREAT TYTHES, ESTATE & MANSION, *SURREY.*

PARTICULARS

OF A

SINGULARLY BEAUTIFUL

FREEHOLD ESTATE,

CONTAINING ABOUT

THREE THOUSAND FIVE HUNDRED ACRES,

WITH THE

MANORS OF ADDINGTON AND TEMPLE,

AND

A CAPITAL STONE BUILT MANSION,

SEATED IN A PARK OF ABOUT

TWO HUNDRED AND TWENTY ACRES,

WITH

Rich diversified Prospects, ornamental Woods and Plantations, in the Centre of a fine
SPORTING COUNTRY, ABOUNDING WITH GAME,

THIRTEEN MILES FROM LONDON,

NEAR CROYDON,

IN THE

COUNTY OF SURREY;

WITH THE

Perpetual Advowson & Great Tythes of the Whole Parish;

Which will be Sold by Auction,

BY MR. SMITH,

AT

GARRAWAY's COFFEE-HOUSE, 'CHANGE-ALLEY, CORNHILL,

On WEDNESDAY, the 7th of JULY, 1802,

AT TWELVE O'CLOCK,

IN ONE LOT,

Advertisement for the auction of Addington Palace

Peak Cottage

The Gazebo

181

Lower Coombe Cottage

Dove Cottage

Copy of painting used as book cover for the American edition and presented by Ron to his PA Helen Chadwick and inscription in a copy of *The Avenue Saga* for her.

THE GAZEBO
PEAK HILL
SIDMOUTH
DEVON
PHONE SIDMOUTH 3308

Dear Helen
Three pages I overlooked. I shan't work on this for weeks so you can have it handy a start on it if you wish.
As Ever
Ronnie

here will tell you that my paperwork wouldn't qualify me
for a remove every other year. No, I've seen myself,
latterly at all events, as a kind of co-ordinator of
all the aims and impulses that keep a place like
Chossdrove alive and useful, and education, in the generally
accepted sense of the word, has never rated very
high on my list of priorities. All that the best of us
can do is to teach boys how to educate themselves
between the time of leaving here, and that Rubicon
that comes, for most of us, at about twenty-five,
when the memory sponge is getting soggy and
we read and forget. "I've had plenty of first-
class scholars through my hands since 1904 but I can't
claim any credit for their academic successes. They
would have been achieved at any school, given the same
material. But helping to equip two generations
of predatory males with the qualities of patience,
tolerance, good fellowship, the ability to
see another's point of view, that I've always seen as
the four keystones of democracy, that's something else and
I'll pipe down now - did I catch a gusty sigh of
relief from the back? - with a final anecdote that came
to mind when I was mulling through the Old Boys'
register this morning, in search of inspiration for
this interminable valediction." It was a very trivial
incident but it must have impressed me at the time, or
why should it have stayed in the mind nearly twenty

Pages 474-476 from the manuscript of *To Serve Them All My Days*
with handwritten corrections

years? It concerned two boys, Pethrick and Rodgers, 'chuff'
who accompanied me when we were travelling over to
When we save
Barcombe by train with to give a charity performance
of that year's opera. It was Christmas time, of course,
naturally and the train was very full. Pethrick, and
finally bagged the last
Rodgers and I found three seats in a compartment
where a young woman was nursing a baby. Within minutes
out
of starting the baby was sick dramatically sick.... ^

— no, no, this
isn't a funny
story, although
perhaps one
aspect of it was.

I remember poor old Chuff Pethrick's expression very
vividly as he took refuge behind my copy of 'The
it was but a thing like that wouldn't
Times'. Upside down. Not that that would bother
Pethrick ☉ Pethrick
Chuff much - He was one of our sky-rockets and went
after leaving us,
on to become the president of a famous insurance
company, and get an O.B.E., and heaven knows what
top-flight/
else they give insurance brokers. I wasn't thinking
But
so much of him, however, but of Chuff Rodgers, who had
chuff

Always
unlucky,
old Chuff he had

^been sitting directly opposite the poor woman and was
thus on the receiving end. of the business. He

*
I didn't know
what to do but
Chuff did.

whipped out a handkerchief - the only clean handkerchief
with
I'd ever seen him sport - and leaned across & wiped
the baby's face and the mother's lap. And After that
we had a tolerably uneventful journal, with Rodgers
making suitable soothing noises to the baby all the
way to the junction.

*
When I say 'wiped'
I mean wiped. It
wasn't a dab, it
was a ministration.
Nothing ostentatious
about it either.

"Now some of you might think that is a damp squib
pretty
friends
to conclude the kind of display we have had here
tonight but it isn't really. Its very relevant, to me

at anyrate, ~~try that~~ we've all been occupied with up
here on the moor all these years. For Rodgers, bless
his thick skull, never won a prize or a race in his
life, and he didn't have time to do ~~what~~ he was ~~clearly~~
equipped to do, raise a family. He was killed three
years later ~~at First Ypres~~, but I still remember him
rather better than I remember Petherick, and I thought of
him ~~this morning~~ as one of our ~~notable~~ successes".

[STOR HERE]

He may well have intended saying more but nobody
gave him the chance, Perhaps because the story was so
thoroughly typical of Algy it released an emotional
response in the audience that could only be vented in a
~~storm of~~ applause, no one present had ever heard ~~equallsed~~
in Big Hall, ~~and~~ David, joining in, forgot to notice
whether or not ~~Rodgers had dented~~ the armour of Alcock's
implacability, ~~And~~ then, remembering him, he glanced that
way again and ~~was had a momentary certainty~~ that Rodgers'
handkerchief had achieved what all Algy's jokes and sly
nudges had failed to achieve. ~~for~~ Alcock had unfolded his
arms, and ~~was glancing downwards instead of straight~~
~~fixedly ahead.~~ It was only when ~~he stood up~~ he realised
he had been mistaken, ~~for~~ Alcock's head came up sharply like
a stork's ~~nushing as~~, tidily, ~~and~~ perfunctorily, he replaced
the table napkin that had fallen when Algy lifted the
water beaker. His long fingers patted its folds and then,
as he refolded his arms, the ~~fixed stare the full length of~~
~~the hall was resumed.~~

OVER.

DELDERFIELD AND THE PUBLISHING WORLD

It was the time of small, independent publishers and Ron found in Hodder & Stoughton a company who was willing to take risks. It had started with Matthew Hodder, aged fourteen, going to work for Mssrs. Jackson & Walford. In 1861, the firm became Jackson, Walford & Hodder and in 1868, when Mssrs Jackson & Walford retired, Matthew Hodder recruited Thomas Wilberforce Stoughton to join him and thus Hodder & Stoughton was born.

At first they were known to publish mainly religious titles, but soon the adventurous spirit took over and they did not shy away from controversial works such as Omar Khayyam's *Rubaiyat* and later Lewis Carroll's *Alice's Adventures in Wonderland.* In 1992 Hodder & Stoughton were taken over by Headline and are now working under the umbrella of Hachette Livre UK and the Managing Director Jamie Hodder-Williams.

R.F. Delderfield was introduced to Hodder & Stoughton by John Attenborough. *God is an Englishman* sat for a year on the Hodder & Stoughton desk because the book was so long. It was unimaginable at the time, that anyone, least of all the then main outlet for books, the libraries, would pay 42 shillings for a hardback book when the usual price would have been around 15 shillings.

Finally Simon and Schuster came in to help with the finance and the novel became a roaring success in the USA. The publication of the saga was a first in the publishing world

I had the good fortune of meeting two of the Hodder men who had been working closely with Ron: One was his editor, Robin Denniston and the other in charge of sales and PR, Eric McKenzie.

Eric invited me to his beautiful country cottage in Mayfield in Sussex. He was the epitome of an English gentleman, chivalrous, charming and with a twinkle in his eye. We had a wonderful afternoon with Eric and his lovely wife Pauline, all of us becoming quite elated with Eric's memories of trips with Ron, often seized by helpless laughter at the thought of some mishaps or bon mots.

Eric took Ron on tours around the country on PR exercises, book signing sessions and interviews with newspapers, radio and television. The two colleagues got on so well that the initial affinity developed into friendship. To their delight, Hodder paid for luxurious hotel accommodation like the Grosvenor House Hotel in London, or the Midlands Hotel in Manchester, or the Queen's Hotel in Leeds, where they enjoyed relaxing in the evenings with a large brandy, a cigarette and a chat about the business of literature, J.B. Priestley and Dickens, Ron's favourite authors.

The trips were never boring:

One night there was a knock on Ron's door. A commotion and heated discussion ensued. It turned out that the bearded Frenchman outside and his TV crew wanted to film something about Dartmoor Prison; it was to do with one of Ron's Napoleonic novels and they came to an agreement to meet on the following morning. Eric could only shake his head.

At a literary lunch attended by various dignitaries, Eric found Ron hotly discussing Victorian drains and sewage systems with the man sitting next to him. As a way of an apology Ron conceded: 'I am a story teller, not a historian,' before being dragged away.

Even when they were not travelling, they kept in close contact. One night Ron phoned Eric to tell him that he had just been shot but that his mother Mary (which was Eric's mother's real name), the school teacher, had survived – of course he was talking about the story he was working on. Eric suspected that he was Pte McTavish.

On another occasion, a distressed and harassed Ron let him know over the phone that he had just dropped a bomb on some of the more unpleasant characters of the Avenue to get rid of them.

In Hodder's London offices colleagues knew that Ron used to swim in the sea each morning with his dog. Often – just when he was towelling himself dry – the manager of the local WH Smith would appear in his black coat and striped trousers with books for the author to sign.

Sadly, neither Eric nor Pauline are with us anymore; in fact Pauline had been quite ill at the time of my visit – I would never have guessed.

****

The second Hodder & Stoughton man I met was Ron's editor Robin Denniston. He has written many books himself, specialising in biographies.

I had written to Robin who to my surprise invited me and my husband to lunch at the Rectory at Little Tew near Oxford. The location was so remote that we had great trouble finding it. A lovely Rayburn stew was welcoming us when we finally arrived.

After lunch, my husband excused himself to explore the delightful hamlet of Little Tew and to give me time to interview Robin about R.F. Delderfield. Robin showed me the Nelson Mandela biography he was just working on, and I waited politely for the moment when I could turn to my subject and the questions I had prepared. Suddenly, Robin proclaimed that this was the hour of his afternoon nap and that I should leave my manuscript and folders with him and pick them up the following week. Considering that we had travelled 150 miles, that wasn't feasible. Watching in astonishment Robin disappearing up the old oak stairs, I was wondering whether I was meant to wait. So I wandered into the corridor – both entrance and back door were wide open. Through the back I glimpsed a wildly overgrown garden with an empty swimming pool.

After about a quarter of an hour I decided that I had outstayed my welcome, grabbed my things and stepped out into the country lane. Opposite the house began a narrow path framed by unruly hedges through which peeped the little church of which Robin had become the rector after his retirement from Hodder.

I turned left towards the hamlet's centre and soon met my husband who was mightily surprised that my audience with the great man had ended already. We were both bemused.

Robin Denniston was certainly a character larger than life and would have been an enormous support for someone like Ron who was compelled to write long family stories at a time when no one had published hundreds of pages in one book. I can just see him defending the author and wielding the red pen to make some cuts.

The letters below give an insight into Ron's and Robin's working relationship and the world of publishing at the time.

Coincidentally, the rector of my Exmoor village moved a couple of years ago to exactly the same rambling old vicarage at Little Tew. It was rather fun to watch his face when I told him that I knew exactly where he was moving to and that I had had lunch there with its previous occupant.

Over the years Robin has been most supportive and complimentary about *Butterfly Moments* and I was sad to hear that he has now passed away.

Jan 3rd. 65.

My Dear Robin,

Re your last letter. I feel that, apart
from the attached, I you could do a far better job on
this than I could; I'm punch drunk on that book and I
feel a new mind is needed to put it over in a brochure. I
agree with you about a quote from the text but perhaps
the same object would be achieved by taking possibly
three dramatic paragraphs from different sections and
quoting them, viz :-

Henry Pitts (description) ...para quote from his
                                 meeting with German troops on
                                 Nov. IIth. I9I8

   Grace Craddock. (description)

                          ...para quote from the
                          suffragette riot.

                ETC.

            I hope to God something comes of this
book. I can't last out much longer and have already
made enquiries about returning to journalism and seeking
a regular job somewhere.

Good wish for 1966.

As Ever & every

Ronnie

P.S. How did Clifford get his book seen &
occupied by Sinatra before publication?
I wish I knew the truth.

191

G. P. PUTNAM'S SONS

200 MADISON AVENUE · NEW YORK 16, N. Y.

Miss Herion
o attach to
pub slip?

March 23, 1965

Robin Denniston, Esq.
Hodder and Stoughton Ltd.
St. Paul's House
Warwick Square
London E.C.4, England

Dear Robin:

I wonder if you've read all five volumes of Ronnie Delderfield's novel
ONE MAN WENT TO MOW? If so, I'm most interested to know what your reaction is.

I'll tell you mine - and that is that I rather rue the day I urged him
to go forth and write a big, broad canvas novel for the American market.
It seems to me that Ronnie has confused his dimensions; his depth is linear - through the generations rather than across the canvas. There's
nothing wrong with the novel, but I'm a little bit dubious about our a-
bility to sell a novel of that length.

Now I'd like to hear from you.

Best regards,

Walter J. Minton

WJM/cp

Peak Cottage,
Sidmouth. April 2nd. 65

My Dear Robin,

     I have worked closely on your basis
and expanded. You can, of course, cut and shape where
you like. I mst say I like writing my own notices! I
also wish you were reviewing for the Times Lit. Sup.
The important thing, I feel, is to convey the sweep and
range of this novel, without forgetting to counteract the
prejudice some readers have against rural themes, with the
promise of comedy and romance. Even the old dears who potter
along to the library nowadays expect sex frankly discussed
in their books and if this is presented within the terms
of marriage they can satisfy their unquiet consciences whilst
enjoying it! We also - in projecting the book - ought to make
the very most of its patriotic thrust as a counterblast to
current sick humour and purely destructive satire. I do not
apologise for the chauvinistic slant herein; it has always seemed
to me that England has given more generously to humanity than
any other nation, that the Ehglish were the first to willingly
take on the kind of responsibilities Paul accepted for his
valley tenants and craftsmen. This, in fact, is the underlying
theme of the book and I feel it will find many unexpected
champions anxious to react against the blatent materialism of
the 'sixties. If I can help in any other way don't hesitate to
let me know.
     I hope, soon, to begin taking the story on into
the Second World War, the stale 'fifties and the Profumo 'sixties
with, perhaps, a slant on the common market situation. But that
is all in the future. It might help you, however, to know I have
detailed plans for this and will probably disappear again into
the Sorrel Valley for another two years! It was a fearsome task
and came close to prostrating me but I mst say I got as much as
I gave from these characters, as indeed I did from the Avenue
people and Jan and Diana in 'Fair Maid'.

     Will you ask your despatch dept. to send on the
following books. Summer is coming and I sell quite a few in my
antique shop.

As Ever
Ronnie

'March 36'   2 cBies.
'Under Enplish
   Sky'   3   ,,
'Fair Maid'   3   ,,
'Unjust Skie'   2   ,,
'Ben fund'   3   ,,
'The Sermon'   1   ,,
'Avenue Stry   2   ,,

June Ist

My Dear Tam,

I took one of my own copies to the
Express and Echo, are local people here with a huge
circulation in the West. This was the result which I
think you might not have. There was a magnificent one
in the Western Morning News and I don't know whether
you heard the Books and Bookman Talk last night on the
Light Programme. It was the best review I've ever
heard and I was delighted. I am getting a copy from
them. The general review situation seems to be
improving and I am rather surprised to find that the
highbrows like the book — something I didn't expect.
I think if we keep pushing with this and quote the
reviews from all sources we ought to build it into a
classic-type library non-fiction book. I hope Hodder's
are pleased with the result so far.

Let me have any reviews I am unlikely to
get.

As Ever
Ronnie

I enclose a letter from Horrocks.
I don't think the old so-and-so
deserves a copy!

(Delderfield)

Peak Cottage.
Peak Hill.
Sidmouth.
June 6. 65

My Dear Robin,

You probably received the script of my Women's Hour talk on the book. It seems to have been successful. I shall be going on again soon in an author vs librarian discussion. I have also sent them – at their request – copies of 'Sermon' & 'Nap. in Love'. They might read one over the air.

I enclose a slip to pass on to the Despatch Dept. In the meantime, could you send one to H.A. Boyer, the C. Schools Inspector we have dealt with before – a copy of 'Under an English Sky' for publicity. He gets around to hundreds of schools – is an old pal of mine & a great fan. He did us a lot of good with previous books. His address is :– 17 St Edmunds Drive, Stanmore, Middx.

As Ever
Ronnie D

9/6/65

You can use any of talk material for promotion

continued overleaf

so much of it being the most expensive. I think Pitman (who will probably like it) should be met & primed well in advance. He & I always see eye to eye & I occasionally write to him. Remember too Pottersman was in at the birth.

As Ever.

Ronnie

Note new address <u>after</u> Sept 30. It is only 30 yds from old one — a coach-house on edge of cliff. I think we might use this also — it is on the site of the spot where Queen Vic's father caught his death of cold in 1819 & is like a Martello tower. The study commands a 30 mile sea vista & the house is probably nearer the sea than any house save a lighthouse in Britain. The BBC TC West are shooting it (& me at work) as soon as we are settled in. But we must spend a day or so together. Why not come down here? We could talk in peace & I could show you the background of the book.

The Gazebo,

DEAR COTTAGE

PEAK HILL
SIDMOUTH
DEVON
PHONE SIDMOUTH 3308

Oct. 25. 65

My Dear Robin,

I have recently been
in touch with several English teachers
& was surprised to learn they had
read 'Adv. of Ben Gunn' to their classes
doing 'Treasure Island'. It struck me
that the Hodder traveller who
calls with school books could put
this forward as an obligatory sequel
&, as you know, the sales of 'text'
books can proliferate, to our mutual
profit. Could you follow this up? It
is already in N. Zealand schools.

I had a good idea today
in this sphere. Suppose I wrote a
book of modern history on the period
1914 — 64, stressing customs crises,
trends etc with a 'light, informative'
slant for children 12-15? I have
done a great amount of research for the

continued overleaf

"...aga & I feel I could present something new in presentation — spicing the bread with a little humourous jam! Would this have any chance? Have you an Emir of Educational Books at St Paul's House? If so could I meet him & put my ideas over?

Touching future promotion. Today I had a very flattering letter out of the blue from Peter Cushing. He seems to be a great fan of mine. Ought he to go on the list of advance copies for a 'quest'?

Another idea I had was this: I am on very friendly terms with Bonham-Carter & Jeremy Thorpe & have campaigned for both. The saga contains an exposition of the Old Liberal Dream. Could we get noisy puffs from them or would B. Carter being a publisher preclude this?

As Ever.

Ronnie

Dec 8.

PEAK COTTAGE
PEAK HILL
SIDMOUTH
DEVON
PHONE SIDMOUTH 308

Oct. 30. 65

My Dear Robin,

An awful situation. A long-standing B.B.C. (TV) appearance has materialised on Tues. owing to factors entirely outside my control. It is being recorded a day before it should have been. & is a networked programme. Can you possibly come later in week? If you want to ring get through to new number (SID 3308) between 1.15 & 2.15. today (Monday) or after 6.30. p.m. I go into hospital for an op. on Nov. 9th for 10 days. After that I have cancelled all engagements away from here for the month.

As Ever
Ronnie

199

9th December, 1965

R. F. Delderfield, Esq.,
The Gazebo,
Peak Cottage,
Peak Hill,
Sidmouth, Devon.

Dear Ronnie,

          I was very glad that Robin Denniston had a chance
of talking with you yesterday and he has told me about your
present problems and future hopes. I was truly sorry to
hear of your family problems as I know how worrying and
distracting they are. We all hope that they may speedily
resolve themselves and our thoughts are very much with you.
But then your own very unpleasant operation must have taken
its toll, though I am glad to hear that you are well on the
road to recovery.

          This note is just to say how very much we are
behind you with A HORSEMAN RIDING BY, and that we hope we
shall jointly be able to make a success of it and that it
will earn our keep satisfactorily for us all. Robin also
mentioned the thought that is in the back of all our minds
that you may well be able to fill the gap left by the death
of Howard Spring. This is, of course, not a matter of imit-
ation, as your style and ways of thinking and his are so very
different, but people who go to libraries and bookshops and
want a good read will be as delighted with your books as with
his, I have no doubt. So, if we can all be thinking and
planning towards your producing a major novel for delivery
say at Christmas each year, for publication in October of
the year after, we might well be able to settle down to a
rhythm of publishing which will benefit us all. Quite honestly

                                             /Cont....

          about half the length of A HORSEMAN RIDING BY is still a
very long book and about 576 pages is a good length. As
to subjects and themes, we would be delighted to discuss
these with you at an early stage so that we know we are
thinking on the same lines.

          I am so sorry you cannot come to our party, but
quite understand the reasons.

          John sends his affectionate regards,

                                   Yours ever,

55, Primley Road,

Sidmouth,

Devon.

Tel: Sidmouth 3179.

11th October, 1969.

Messrs. Hodder & Stoughton, Ltd.,
St. Paul's House,
Warwick Lane,
London, E.C.4.

Dear Sirs,

Mr. R.F. Delderfield.

I have been asked by Mr. Delderfield to advise you that he
will be on holiday as from tomorrow, 12th October, until Tuesday, 21st
October.

Should you have any urgent reason to get in touch with him,
he asks that you should write to me and I will 'phone him.   He feels
this will be the quickest way, as he expects to be out during the
day.

Yours sincerely,

(Mrs. H. Chadwick)

55, Primley Road,

Sidmouth,

Devon, EX10 9LF.

27th July, 1972.

Mr. R. Denniston,
Messrs. Hodder & Stoughton Ltd.,
Saint Paul's House,
Warwick Lane,
London, EC4P 4AH.

Dear Mr. Denniston,

Thank you very much for the copy of TO SERVE THEM ALL MY DAYS.
Ronnie usually gave me a copy of his books but as this was published
at such a sad time I did not have one.

I was very sorry to miss the service but my sister, Margaret Patient,
attended and telephoned me to tell me all about it and also sent me a
copy of the Service Sheet.   She also told me how kind Hodders were
to invite her back for the buffet meal after the service and that she
very much enjoyed meeting several of the people connected with Hodders.

TO SERVE THEM ALL MY DAYS means very much to me as Ronnie used my
husband's nickname "CHAD", coupled with the surname of a very dear friend
of his, to name one of the major characters.   He always enjoyed exchanging
bandinage with him and visits about script often developed into discussions
covering a wide field.

Once again, thank you for your kind thought.

Yours sincerely,

55, Primley Road,
Sidmouth,
Devon, EX10 9LF.

9th August, 1972.

Mr. E. McKenzie,
Messrs. Hodder & Stoughton Ltd.,
Saint Paul's House,
Warwick Lane,
London, EC4P 4AH.

Dear Mr. McKenzie,

When I saw you at Exeter you asked me whether Ronnie had said anything about a dedication in his last book GIVE US THIS DAY. I replied that he hadn't but that I would speak to May and find out if she knew anything.

When May came home from Veronica's she came up to see me with a lifelong friend, and I mentioned the dedication. May did not seem to know anything about it, but said if Ronnie had discussed it with you she supposed it would be all right. Her friend, however, seemed to think that the last book written should be dedicated to his wife, and I know May would be very happy if it were so.

I went to see May yesterday and discussed it with her again as I have sent off the scripts to Mr. Denniston, and she feels that you must decide to whom the book should be dedicated. If I may, I should like to put forward a suggestion, which is that if the book is dedicated as you understood it was to be, perhaps Hodders could put in a paragraph or two stating that it was solely due to his wife's devoted and loving nursing and encouragement that the book was finished.

This has been a difficult letter for me to write, but I do understand how May feels - she wants to respect Ron's wishes to you but would, I know, be heartened by the fact of his last book having some mention of her.

Yours sincerely,

Helen Schadwick

55, Primley Road,
Sidmouth,
Devon, EX10 9LF.

9th August, 1972.

Mr. R. Denniston,
Messrs. Hodder & Stoughton Ltd.,
Saint Paul's House,
Warwick Lane,
London, E.C.4.

Dear Mr. Denniston,

I have today posted to you four parcels containing the two scripts of Ronnie's book, GIVE US THIS DAY. Parcels 1 and 2 contain your copy which you annotated and which I have incorporated into Ronnie's script and his alterations and deletions into yours.

Mr. McKenzie spoke to me in Exeter about the dedication, and I shall be writing to him about this.

The rough map I found in Ronnie's papers I have placed in the front of the top copy, but I doubt whether it is enough to make a complete map from.

Perhaps you will let me know when the parcels have arrived.

Yours sincerely,

DAVID HIGHAM ASSOCIATES, Ltd.

Authors' Agents.

Telephone: 01-437 7888.
Telegrams: HIGHLIT, WESDO, LONDON.
Cables: HIGHLIT, LONDON-W1

5-8, LOWER JOHN STREET,
GOLDEN SQUARE,
LONDON, W1R 4HA

DIRECTORS:
DAVID HIGHAM Managing
BRUCE HUNTER
JACQUELINE KORN
ANTHONY CROUCH

Michael Levin,

Mrs Helen Chadwick
55 Primley Road
Sidmouth
Devon EX10 9LF

31st October 1972

Dear Mrs Chadwick,

Thank you for your letter of October 26th. As you say it will be difficult indeed for you to find a relationship with another author anything like what you had with Ronnie Delderfield. Morever, I'm afraid we don't ever use outside typists ourselves, though occasionally authors ask us to recommend someone and we would be very glad to recommend you to any West Country author. What does occur to me however is that it might be worth your while getting in touch with David & Charles the Newton Abbot firm as they might well have some outside work they could give you. They are a big company now and I hope they'll be able to provide something for you. I should write if I were you to Mrs Pamela Thomas.

With kind regards.

Yours sincerely,

Bruce Hunter

BH/tf

HODDER AND STOUGHTON LIMITED

SAINT PAUL'S HOUSE WARWICK LANE LONDON EC4P 4AH Telephone 01-248 5797

Telegrams and Cables EXPOSITOR LONDON EC4

RAD/FA

26th January 1973

Mrs. H. Chadwick,
55 Primley Road,
Sidmouth,
Devon,
EX10 9LF

Dear Mrs. Chadwick,

I am writing to say that proofs of GIVE US THIS DAY are due on
March 15th and I would like to give you an opportunity of reading
these and letting us have any corrections that you note. They
would need to be back in this office by March 28th. Mrs. Delderfield
has given permission for this. Additionally we will read the book
for press ourselves, here, and will check it very carefully, but I
know how much you worked, particularly on this book with Ronnie,
and hope you will like to take on this extra job.

Yours,

For Katlin Rennisha

55, Primley Road,
Sidmouth,
Devon, EX10 9LF.

Your ref. RAD/FA.   27th January, 1973.

Mr. R. Denniston,
Messrs. Hodder & Stoughton Ltd.,
Saint Paul's House,
Warwick Lane,
London, EC4P 4AH.

Dear Mr. Denniston,

        In your letter dated 26th January you asked whether I would
like to take on "this extra job"!   I have not tried very hard to
obtain similar work as I think it is rather impossible in the South West.

        I should therefore be very pleased to read the proofs of GIVE US THIS
DAY and will check it with any notes I made whilst Ronnie was alive.

        I assume you will accept responsibility for the return postage and
that you will be kind enough to let me have a copy of the book when
printed.

                        Yours sincerely,

BOSTON UNIVERSITY

R.F. Delderfield took a long time to visit his fans in the United States of America. Many were 'expats' from the West Country who adored reading about the England they had left behind.

Once there, Ron couldn't praise the American hospitality and warmth highly enough. When Boston University asked him whether he would like to make a modest contribution to their 'Special Collections' department he donated all the notebooks and original manuscripts which he had not yet given away to friends and family or discarded. The collection is still there, 30 boxes, and R.F. Delderfield is firmly on the students' 'to read list' in their English department. Ron had been surprised and saddened that an American University had taken more interest in his work than any British institution. Of course, he felt flattered and willing to oblige.

A letter to an American fan, Mrs. Share, January 15th 1969

Boston University

Department of Special Collections
771 Commonwealth Avenue
Boston, Massachusetts 02215
Tel: 617/353-3696
Fax: 617/353-2838

March 31, 1998.

Mrs. Marion Lindsey-Noble
Tryst
#4 Burlings Lane
Knockholt
Kent
TN147PB
ENGLAND

Dear Mrs. Lindsey-Noble:

Thank you for your letter dated February 27, 1998. I am happy that the Delderfield Inventory was so warmly received.

Unfortunately, I cannot fulfill your request to have copies made of any correspondence from the collection. The restrictions which bind us also protect the material as unique, and keep them available for all scholars to use.

I did set one of our assistants to the task of answering your other questions. After reviewing some of the material in the collection, I may report the following:

After the release of *God is an Englishman,* Delderfield did a tour of the U.S.A. including New York and Chicago, circa summer-fall, 1970, [based on a newspaper interview]. *Englishman* was a US bestseller; according to Simon & Schuster, it sold 60,000 copies in hardcover, and 500,000 in paperback. *Theirs Was the Kingdom* was also a bestseller, though it did not reach the proportions of *Englishman.*

I hope this information is useful to you. Please let me know if there is anything else I may do to assist you.

Sincerely yours,

Sean D. Noel
Public Service Administrator

A letter from Sean Noel of Boston University

R.F. DELDERFIELD IN HIS OWN WORDS

This is the moment when I leave you entirely in the hands of the Master:

EVENING STANDARD   Tuesday October 21st 1958.
Review by R F Delderfield

Mr. Ponsonby ends an old rumour:

The Lost Duchess by D.A.Ponsonby, Chapman & Hall 18s.

This is the story of young, eager Louise, ill-starred mother of the practical idealist who married Queen Victoria and who, by dying unexpectedly in 1861, plunged Britain into semi-mourning that endured 40 years.
   The author relies, in the main, on Louise's spate of girlish letters to her friend and confidante, Augusta von Studnitz.
   Happiness
   Through these letters we trace the pattern of Louise's ecstatic marriage to Duke Ernest of Saxe-Coburg, her slow disillusionment, her giddy round of pleasures to replace the lost love, and her ultimate divorce.
   The Duchess found bried happiness with a second husband, who she also loved to distraction. When she died, aged 31, she is said to have decreed that her husband was to carry her embalmed corpse with him wherever he went!
   So far routine biography. But this book is much, much more than that. It is a shutter-peep into the early evening of what one might call "antimacassar feudalism".
   Mr. Ponsonby also disposes of the 100 year old rumour that Albert was illegitimate. Louise would certainly have confessed "Darling Augusta"

R.F. Delderfield considers the vital role of the English police in the '70s.

THOSE of us whose memories extend to the days of the First World War can recall a time (it seems incredibly distant now) when the English thought of their national security as being entirely dependent upon a fleet of ironclads and a host of jolly Jack Tars. The latter were prone to be invested with glamour of the kind now lavished on an assortment of public entertainers.

The Royal Navy, in those days, was not so much a service as a cult. It was not in the least unusual for girls and boys to appear in public with gold-lettered hatbands reading HMS Arethusa or HMS Goliath, and this nearworship of the fleet persisted into the 1920's, for we saw it as the means that had enabled us to sustain a four-year conflict with an immeasurably superior enemy, and the guardian of the realm in any future war.

For my part I still feel in need of a shield of some kind, not to protect me from becoming the victim of knavish tricks in foreign chancellories but, as it were, from danger within, from ourselves if you like, for it is not an exaggeration to say that the entire social fabric of this country now rests on a single body of trained men just as it did generations ago, and I wonder how many of us are fully aware of this, or pay more than lipservice to a grossly overworked (and, to my mind, grossly underpaid) police force that alone prevents the disintegration of our way of life in England.

Thus, from time to time, I feel disposed to take up the truncheon, in lieu of the cudgel, and lay about me a little, in the hope that others will join me in acknowledging this profoundly disturbing fact – i.e. that the morale of the police force is every bit as vital to us in 1970 as was the Royal Navy in 1588, 1805, 1914 and 1939.

THREE APPROACHES

There exists, in England today, three distinct approaches to the familiar figure of the polite, unobtrusive men who can be seen going about their work in any community between Land's End and John o'Groats. There is the person who respects and accepts them as an essential pillar of our society; the person who, having enlisted himself or herself in the lunatic fringe, regards them unequivocally as public enemies; and the person who regards them much as he is wont to regard a town hall or a lamp-standard, that is to say, as part of the local scenery.

Of these sections of opinion the latter is by far the strongest and most steadfast in its outlook. Those subscribing to it seem persuaded that, having donned a helmet and a blue uniform, and saddled himself with the prefix 'Constable' in exchange for 'Mr.' a young man has opted out of the human family and become, in effect, a kind of animated machine, with no emotions to speak of, no real friends, no social obligations apart from obeying the orders of superiors (themselves dehumanised long ago), and no needs as an ordinary man seeking some kind of amiable contact with his neighbours.

It is an aspect of English life that completely baffles me, as a person who has worked with, and come to know, a large number of policemen, for it extends to no other class of citizen, not even the thugs these men spend much of their time catching and hauling up before authorities who, as like as not, urge them to be good boys and turn them loose again to plan some fresh outrage on our persons and property.

Isn't it long past the time when we reversed this approach and made some attempt to integrate the police into our awareness. Not merely respect them, as some of us already do, but give them the kind of trust and comradeship we gave sailors in the days when we relied on navies?

Another curious fallacy persists among the general public concerning policemen. They are deemed, poor devils, to have been born entirely without a sense of humour, and whilst they are sometimes seen to be compassionate, and are expected to be fearless, infallible and beyond human temptation, they are not really regarded as the kind of chaps one should pass the time of day with unless, of course, one has just been relieved of one's private property, or affronted by someone who has decided to throw away the rule book.

I think this state of affairs will have to change dramatically in the next year or so unless we are to stand by and see the nation slide into the kind of anarchy witnessed in Northern Ireland last summer, or Paris not so long ago, or any one of a dozen communities right across the world where the louts take over, shouting one mindless slogan or another as John Citizen, wringing his hands, wonders what has happened to the law and order that he, his father and his grandfather once took for granted.

For, let's face it, the point of no return is not far distant. Almost every day over the last 12 months we have seen stupid, pointless and often brutal violence erupt on the streets, and the steady growth of a curious animal who seems to find fulfilment in smashing, kicking, yelling, bullying, tormenting and crusading in the name of a cause that he cannot even explain to himself, much less those exercising authority in our cities, towns and villages.

HOW IT HAPPENS

It is quite useless to claim that the number of young people who fall into the hippy grade, or the rowdy grade, are an extremely small percentage of England's youth. This is quite true, of course, but what the apologist does not tell you is that it does not need more than a small percentage of louts in one assembly, be it protest march, football crowd, or downtown Saturday-nightlarkers to convert that assembly into a maelstrom, mostly composed of people trying to get clear of it.

A few dozen inarticulate young savages have, times without number, reduced a football excursion train to a shambles, and 50 such misfits can quite easily terrorise a seaside town for hours. And on these occasions it is always the police who are called upon to restore order, and invariably do restore order, without resorting to the tactics of foreign police under similar pressures.

My argument is that this is just not good enough.

When public disorder erupts in front of his eyes all able-bodied democrats should have a go one way or another, backing the police force on the spot if they can, and giving any kind of information that will assist in arresting the ringleaders, or bearing witness at any subsequent appearance in court.

Stories concerning public violence that are coming out of America every day are some indication of what can happen when the police operate alone. It is well known that the American citizen will do almost anything to avoid becoming 'involved' in a public disorder of any kind, and I find the word very curious, for the fact is we are all very much involved in what is happening with mounting frequency on our streets, at our football matches, and often on our beaches during Bank Holidays.

The extent of our involvement, however, should go far beyond co-operating with the police wherever and whenever we can, that is to say, by having a go ourselves, or by keeping our wits about us and passing on to the police anything we notice that might assist them in the performance of their duty.

We should – by bombarding our M.P.s and newspapers and by putting pointed questions on the subject of public order to every candidate who solicits our vote – strive to bring about an entirely different climate in England as regards this descent to anarchy.

We need an abrupt halt in any further legislation that tends to widen the so-called permissive society. We need the imposition by all courts of far stiffer penalties for all displays of public violence and assaults upon the police.

An even greater need is to refurbish, not so much the image of the police we hear so much about these days, but our own image, as a nation that once took pride in its claim to be safe, sane and law-abiding.

LEADERS HAVE FAILED US

To my mind our leaders have failed us lamentably in this respect during the last year or so. The Home Secretary has spoken up recently but not so long ago the Chancellor of the Exchequer, no less, was telling us that a permissive society was a civilised society. He should, I feel, have found a different adjective.

Barmy, brutal or decadent would have been a better choice.

In the meantime one of our prominent Liberals appeared on television a few days ago openly supporting the sitting-down on football pitches as a means of combating racial prejudice in South Africa. He ought not to have to be reminded that such displays have had two almost inevitable results. The overworked police has had another job on its hands and scuffles have broken out resulting in yet more public violence.

All these side-issues have a bearing, I feel, on the disarray of our present society but none more so than our need to change our subconscious belief that a policeman is a man set apart.

He isn't.

He is one of us and today he needs more than an occasional pat on the back, or a word or two of praise from the magistrate, or leader-writer.

He needs the trust and friendship of every man and woman in these islands who is prepared to fight back against the violent and the sloppy-minded, against the Hippy, the squatter, the thug, the vandal and the lout. For these people are doing their damndest to destroy a way of life it took the English a thousand years to perfect.

And the only agency to prevent them doing just that is the policeman.

With your help.

SO MANY ENGLANDS
RFD finds many facial changes, but the country's soul remains the same.

Two YEARS AGO I sat down at this desk to make a map. It was a map of England and Wales, in the year 1857, the starting point of a 674 page saga concerning the adventures of a midVictorian haulier who hitched his capital to a fleet of waggons that were to bring him fame and fortune. I entitled my latest novel God is an Englishman – at the risk of affronting the Race Relations Board – not because I claim to have seen the Almighty's passport, but because it is the story of an era when the Englishman really did believe God beamed upon his commercial and imperialistic ventures. Seven weeks ago, on the day the book was published, I was required by my publisher to embark on a 3,000 mile journey over my hero's Victorian routes and into most of his regional depots, as a promotion tour of the book.

'Come and see how it has changed', he said genially.

I went reluctantly. The weather was vile, spring slipping back into the bondage of winter, and I was already deep in the saga's sequel, carrying the story up to 1890.

For all that it proved one of the most rewarding and instructive journeys of my life.

I noticed the changes in England, and outwardly they were immense, almost too staggering to be contemplated. Yet there were areas where there were virtually no changes at all and two of them solaced me as a writer, inseparably bound up with the destinies of the British tribes. One such area seemed to me of paramount importance. It was the essential characteristics of the British – perhaps the one field where my hero, *Adam Swann*, born 1827, would have felt at home and among friends.

THE LONDON SCENE
They will tell you on TV and elsewhere that the British have lost confidence in themselves. To me, back from meeting hundreds of Britons of all ages, and in areas as far apart as the Border, the North Foreland and the Western peninsula, this is no more than a fashionable fiction.

An author's promotion tour follows a complicated pattern. Mine involved, among other occasions, three literary luncheons, five booksellers' cocktail parties, 12 radio tape recordings for home and overseas, two TV appearances and 18 press interviews. In the course of my lunges across the length and width of the country I visited London,

Leeds, Manchester, Newcastle, Norwich, Croydon, Birmingham, Exeter and Plymouth, and as I travelled, talked, listened, dozed, caught trains, lost trains, stamped the snow from my shoes and beat my arms to restore circulation, a conviction began to grow on me that this was not the first time round, that I was not, in fact, myself in 1970 but Adam Swann, my haulier hero, making his rounds in a particularly punishing winter around 1860, when his network was well established.

It was as though I was looking at two photographs superimposed upon one another, revealing all manner of contrasts but marked underlying similarities. The contrasts were the landscapes and their apparatus--teeming cities where once sheep had grazed, thundering ten-wheel trucks and 'artics' where three-horse drays and 'growlers' had passed, and this curious double pattern advertised itself wherever I went, north, south, east or west.

South of the River, outside the old George Inn (completely unchanged) I watched the swirl of London traffic, with its accompanying roar and fume, and its frustrating snarl-ups. But really there was nothing new in this. In 1860 horse traffic jams approaching London Bridge were even worse, and in place of the petrol fumes and clash of gears was the acrid, all-pervading stink of horse droppings, and the ceaseless clatter of iron rims on stone setts.

Nor was this all.

Watching the traffic roll I witnessed, time and again, the dreadful patience of the British going about their lawful concerns, a patience that shows itself in that peculiar British institution – the queue. And salting it – as old as London itself – was the ironic quip of the Cockney, that has enabled him to survive not merely a millenium of traffic jams, but far worse ordeals, notably the Blitz and the stalemate of the Western Front in the years 1914-18.

It was down here that I got my first clue of the changelessness and timelessness of England, so that I began to look constantly at the 'superimposed' photographs. It became for me an absorbing game, spotting half-concealed factors, of the kind one finds in the puzzle picture page of a child's comic.

THE NEW WOMEN

One of the major sub-plots of the saga is the emergence of the feminist and the rise of what the Victorians called 'The New Women'.

The New Women, praise God, were in evidence everywhere in 1970. Indeed, I do not know how I should have managed without them. At Newcastle, and again at Leeds and Manchester, almost all the press interviewing and grooming for radio and television appearances, was stage-managed by breathtakingly pretty girls in their early twenties. Their skill, ingenuity and astonishing aplomb, left one wondering whether our national concerns would not be vastly improved by the mass abdication of men. It was with a feeling of awe that I found myself talking into a microphone held by a soft, well-manicured hand, and watching these supremely confident girls handle recording apparatus the way I used to handle a Royal Sovereign pencil in my cubreporting days. I was interviewed by a round dozen of them and they all astonished me by the sure grasp they had of their respective mediums. I never saw a single one of them at a loss. I never saw one flustered or even temporarily checked in her surging approach to problems of technology and communications, so that I thought, *'Adam Swann promoted one such woman to the post of manager of a region. He was an ass. He should have cast around his Leeds and Newcastle depots and recruited a dozen. By 1870 he would have been a millionaire'*.

Echoes of old-time traffic problems in London, and a vision of the triumph of Mrs. Pankhurst's suffrage campaigns in the north-east… but in Manchester, across the snow-bound Pennines, there was fresh confirmation that the face of England changes but the soul is much the same.

In *God is an Englishman* I had written of a Manchester blighted by the cotton famine, brought about by the American Civil War, of a city that resurrected itself to become a challenger of London for the title of 'Capital of the Empire'.

In 1970 I was witnessing a second miracle, for I remember the Manchester of the early Nineteen-Thirties, when King Cotton was dying, and the northern capital along with it. Yet Manchester did not die. Its resilience, its tremendous vitality and inventiveness, nursed it back to its present prosperity, and the keynote of the cure can be expressed in one word-diversification. The Mancunian, putting the past behind him, diversified to such an extent that life went on very much as usual.

Today Manchester is still one of the most prosperous cities of the Western World.

THE COMMUTERS
South-east again, this time to Croydon, where yet another repetitive pattern awaited me. I spent six years of my childhood in a suburb of Croydon, writing of it 40 years later as *The Dreaming Suburb*. And so it was when I went there, in 1918, in some ways as pastoral as Devon.

Down here, of course, the structural changes were immense but the pattern was the same, in spite of the new one-way traffic routes, and the vast building estates spilling across the Kent/Surrey border. It was the commuter pattern, first evident in the march of the mid-Victorian businessmen into the rural villages and leafy lanes of Addiscombe, Shirley, West Wickham, Addington and Bromley where, in 1860, my hero Swann bought a country estate, founded a dynasty and settled for travelling to Southwark every day on the old South Eastern and Chatham railway.

I stood outside East Croydon station and watched the commuter trains spill out their thousands of latterday Adam Swanns, going home after a day's toil to the telly and their weekend gardening. Has all that much changed in 110 years?

And finally, in Norwich, a rare treat. Here I shared a guest speaker engagement with the great-granddaughter of one of my characters, surely a unique privilege. For here, convulsing an audience with wry stories of her life as a literary celebrity in the United States, was Monica Dickens, promoting her latest novel that deals with the work of the Samaritans among potential suicides. The Dickens family haven't changed much either. Its present standardbearer is still concerned with the sores and ailments of society. To get material for this book Monica became a Samaritan. How her great ancestor would have approved!

We have lost an Empire. We have lost, they say, the leadership of the West and with it our identity. But what have we retained in the thirty years since Britain, single-handed for more than a year, held the ring against Nazi barbarism? I can think of things, reminded of them again and again over 3,000 miles of a seven-week journey, and I am proud enough – arrogant enough if you like – to list them. For it seems to me, an unrepentant chauvinist, that they are infinitely more significant than Imperial trappings and what the TV pundits call 'a role' or an 'identity'.

They include compassion, humour, enterprise, ingenuity, a deep concern for law and order, neighbourliness, sanity, self-respect and, above all, a quality of tolerance that does not flourish anywhere else on earth.

Sometime, soon perhaps, those who think Britain is on the way out will acknowledge this. In the meantime why don't we begin by acknowledging it ourselves?

RFD recalls the scents and sounds of nostalgia

WHEN I was around seventeen, and serving time as a cub reporter, I attended a good many lectures I would have dodged if they hadn't been the means of filling an odd column or two on my local weekly. As it was, I was obliged to sit in on many learned discourses, and it was one of those imagined penalties of being young that showed a rich if unlikely profit in middle age. For this is one of the hidden bonuses of newspaper work; you learn things against your will, go places you wouldn't normally go, meet all kinds of people you would go out of your way not to meet if you were say, a bank clerk or a shop assistant. It was that way with me when I started work in the late 'twenties, and I was reminded of the fact when I heard, this week, of the death of the famous jazz band leader, Harry Roy.

Harry Roy probably wouldn't be known to the under thirties, but when I was young he occupied a position roughly equivalent with Tom Jones, or one of the Beatles. His band had a special sound, so that you always knew when it was around, and I later came to associate it with the sound of the era, a haunting combination of throbbing sax, shuffling feet, and background melody obsessed with moons over the various states of the Union, almost a must for a dance number in those happy-go-lucky days.

It was listening to an excerpt of Harry Roy's dance orchestra on the radio that made me think of the vital importance the ear plays in signposting the way back to what H. E. Bates calls, in his autobiography, 'The Vanished World'. It was hearing that beat, evoking so many scenes and faces I had assumed forgotten, that reminded me of one of those lectures I reluctantly attended where I heard something I never did forget, for it was an expert's address on the faculty of memory and the vital part it plays in the lives of every one of us. I remember particularly one phrase that summed up the expert's message. He said: "We never really forget anything. We only think we do. Mostly we don't need more than a particle of what our senses record in any one day on earth, so we file it away and say we have forgotten it. But it is there just the same, waiting for a combination of circumstances, and a special need, to supply the key that will open a particular cabinet in the attics of the brain and let it out."

I don't know who that lecturer was, but he certainly knew his stuff. As a professional writer of fiction and biography, I have more need of those memory cabinets than most people and have been returning to them every day of my working life. But only recently did I learn to appreciate their immense value. For so long, I told myself, I had a fairly good memory and left it at that. I now see that my memory is neither better nor worse than the next man's. It is simply a case of needing it more than he does.

Most people, I imagine, would select the eye as the most important organ of the body when it comes to filling those cabinets in the attics of the brain, but not me. I should be inclined to put the ear and the nose well ahead of the eye, inasmuch as the eye is a far less accurate piece of apparatus when it comes to stocking up.

Take that old friend, for instance, the scent of an autumn bonfire. For me, as for many people I feel, it has the power to conjure up scenes from childhood on the instant. The mere whiff of burning leaves in September or early October is a magic carpet that you occupy willy nilly, to be whirled back across the decades to a time when you were looking about you and forming your own individual estimate of the world about you. Every time I pass an autumn bonfire I see the faces of children I played with in the days immediately following the First World War, in settings I recall with nostalgia now, for almost all of them are covered with between-the-wars housing estates and great arterial roads.

Memory, getting a sly nudge through the nostrils, can be more than nostalgic, however. There have been occasions when it has proved of vital importance to the casual sniffer and I recall one of them, retold in a story about a general on the eve of a battle against an opposite number, whose name he vaguely recalled as that of someone he had known long ago.

I believe Monty is our greatest living apostle of the adage, 'Know your enemy!' (He kept a photograph of Rommel in his caravan during the desert fighting) and it seems that this general was of the same school of thought.

He knew that if he could recall that old acquaintance to mind he could anticipate his moves and win the battle, but he had mislaid the key of that particular filing cabinet until, striking his head on a low bough in an orchard, he jerked an apple loose, picked it up and absently sniffed it.

At once the key slipped into his hand as he recalled a scene from his boyhood in a classroom where the strong smell of apple cores mingled with that of chalk and dust. He remembered the man in question – now fighting on the other side – sized him up, made his own dispositions, and won the battle. Not with men and munitions, but with an apple.

There must be many such instances, and perhaps every reader has his or her own nasal signpost to the past. I can name a good many - hot tar on a country road in summer; wallflowers on a churchyard wall; hyacinths that are always evocative; the curious smell that emerges from new books that invariably evokes the beginning of a new school year; steam-heat, that I will ever associate with my first day in New York where the smell prevails everywhere, except in the nostrils of natives who have got used to it. And that country smell of baking bread that hangs around in all old cottages, years and years after the introduction of the packaged loaf.

There are evocative sounds too. The outer London suburb of my childhood had a special song of its own, a subtle melody made up of clicking shears, the whirr of hand-pushed lawn mowers, and the distant shouts of children at play. The air-raid siren (once known as Moaning Minnie) that still makes my stomach turn over, even though the fire signal is the wartime 'All Clear'. The chatter of typewriters in unison, that takes me back to my first few days in a Commercial College and recalls so many delightful bobbed and shingled heads, that were responsible, alas, for so many botched exercises on my part.

It would be interesting to know whether any *This England* readers have their own nasal and oral signposts to the vanished worlds.

THIS ENGLAND Spring 1972

RFD reveals his New Year prayer to the men at Westminster…

I WAS asked by the Editor to contribute an article to the Spring issue of This England and find myself writing it on New Year's Eve.

It is tempting, on these occasions, to review the past twelve months but it is a temptation I find no difficulty in resisting. 1971, for the British, has been a depressing year. The cost of living has soared, as have the unemployment figures. The nightmare of Ulster is still with us, and does not promise to improve. Neither is the international scene more cheerful. It is therefore more profitable, I feel, to address oneself to the future – that is to say, the future of the English race, for whom this journal caters. And what could be more seasonable, in the final hours of 1971, than to offer a plea amounting almost to a prayer, to our masters in Westminster. My New Year message for them, for what it is worth, is USE 1972 TO MEET THE PEOPLE YOU ARE THERE TO REPRESENT.

In the last few years, indeed throughout the last decade embracing, as it did, a Macmillan government, two Wilson governments and one Heath government, the gulf between governors and governed has been widening month by month. One might almost say day by day, and this is not merely my view, or the view of any other voter currently disenchanted with the way democracy is being practised in Britain, but the view of politicians themselves. How often have we heard them accuse one another, in the TV jargon of the day, of 'loss of credibility' or, occasionally, give voice to a wry admission that 'we don't seem to have put our case across to the electorate'.

Let me compliment them on these signs of self-doubt. Mr. Heath, Mr. Wilson, Mr. Jenkins, Mr. Maudling and whoever else it might concern, you are not altogether credible; you have indeed failed to make your policies understood by a majority of citizens, and proof of this is that most of your decisions seem to be in flat contradiction to the wishes of the people who sent you there and will be asked to do so again at the next parliamentary election. Only rarely, over this period of ten years, have you done anything in the way of law-making or law-adjustment that would meet with the approval of a majority of the voters, and unless you mend your ways in this respect not only you but Westminster itself will cease to be credible. People might even start casting around and find some means of restructuring the whole process of government by the people for the people.

Let us, therefore, glance over our shoulder for a moment and ponder some of the decisions you have made, and are in the process of making, that qualify as acts of contravention against the inclinations and good sense of the man in the street.

Pre-eminent in this list of You-Mightn't-Like-It-But-We-Think-It's-Good-For-You nostrums is, of course, the application to join the Common Market. Even the most devoted disciple of the Treaty of Rome must, by now, be under no illusion that the British, as a whole, hate and fear the merging of their national interests with those of the continental nations. Any housewife in the country will tell you that joining Europe will make further weekly inroads into her housekeeping purse. The small trader, the factory worker, the small farmer, the self-employed and the fishermen of Britain to name only a few groupings would heave a great sigh of relief if, through some fortunate twist in circumstances, we were obliged to back-pedal right now. Yet a majority at Westminster are hellbent in legislating for the minority, carefully marshalled by big business, rather than for the inarticulate majority who are expected to do as they're told and fall into line.

Is this government of the people by the people? I cannot believe that it is, particularly in view of Mr. Heath's election pledge on the subject in June, 1970, a pledge that must have won him the votes of a great number of uncommitted electors.

Now look at the gay dispensation of public money in the last month or two, notably the rises M.P.s awarded themselves, the Lords, and certain members of the Royal Family.

I doubt if there are many among the English who begrudge the Queen and Prince Charles a steep rise, for at least they and Prince Philip can be seen to be doing an excellent job of work for the country.

But what is a man on the dole, or a pensioner struggling to make ends meet, or a young couple scrabbling round to find enough money to put down on a house, to make of the thumping increases awarded to the less active and not so popular members of the Royal family? Not much, I would say, and even less of the news that every attendance of a peer in the House of Lords will bring a daily reward of around eight pounds, ten shillings (old style) and this for men who must be fairly well off, and are well placed to get themselves on a board and pick up a fat salary for about one tenth of the effort a factory worker puts into a monotonous task.

It simply does not make sense to dish out these vast sums of money to people who can well do without it, at a time when at least half the families in the land are having a very hard struggle to get by.

Take another area. There may be a large number of voters in Britain who welcome the prospect of more motorways and new airfields but it is an even bet to say they are outnumbered by others who are beginning to be deeply disturbed by the ravishing of the countryside, once the prettiest in Europe, now fast becoming a complex of suburbs.

Down in the West country there are many who fear the approach of the M4 and what it might mean to their way of life and they are not wholly comforted by bland assurances that this new road will bring industrial prosperity to the area. Hundreds of thousands of elderly people settled down here because of what counties like Devon, Somerset and Cornwall had to offer in the way of peace and quiet. Who really cares a damn about their preferences?

One could go on indefinitely, listing instances where the wishes of ordinary folk, and those of big business and so-called progressives, diverge, all the way from the courageous people of Stansted and Cublington to a steady majority who think the government made a mistake by abolishing capital punishment and thus positively encouraging the use of firearms among criminals.

There are so many more important issues in the purely domestic sphere that should occupy Westminster in 1972. Our hospitals and, even more, our institutions for the mentally sick, mentally handicapped and chronically sick, are in dire need of the money spent on introducing decimal currency, buying our way into Europe, or handing over our cash to the Lords and virtual nonentities.

So I say, to every member of Parliament, in God's name get out and meet your constituents in 1972 and by that I don't mean the party faithful, who organised your club membership up there. I mean the real people who are finding life more and more difficult on a few pounds a week. Listen to what they have to say for it is they, in the main, who will have to find the rise you have just awarded yourselves.

THE BBC, RADIO, TV AND FILMS

Like so many artists before him, R.F. Delderfield became almost more popular after his death than he had ever been in his life time. The English media suddenly woke up to the fact that his sagas were enormously filmable and made wonderful series on TV.

Not that R.F. Delderfield had nothing to do with the media before his death. He had been forever trying to create publicity for his plays and had written many adaptations for the radio. At first, his plays and comedies were broadcast on radio and TV; later on *Worm's Eye View* was turned into a film and in 1958 Ron wrote the script for *Carry On Sargeant*, the first in the Carry On series, which was based on his play *The Bull Boys*. This has now been all a long time ago, but when you read through the cast lists you find names that still ring a bell today: Bob Monkhouse, Dora Bryan, Charles Hawtrey, Hattie Jacques and many others. Ronald Shiner had been the star of *Worm's Eye View* on stage as well as in the film, ably assisted by Garry Marsh, John Blythe and Diana Dors in 1951.

The Dreaming Suburb was shown in 1959 on London Weekend Television under the title *People Like Us* with John Duttine and Jim Norton, but R.F. Delderfield's biggest success came six years after his death when in 1978, the BBC screened a series with Nigel Havers in the lead role as *The Horseman Riding By*. The success was so immediate and huge that two years later, John Duttine starred as David Powlett-Jones, the headmaster of Bamfylde School in another adaptation of a Delderfield novel, *To Serve Them All My Days* and two years later still, a young Patsy Kensit shone as Diana in the series of the same name.

Interviews with the author were revived like BBC2s *Mightier Than The Sword* and Eric McKenzie was asked to put together questions for a candidate on *Mastermind*. She had chosen the novels of R.F. Delderfield as her specialist topic. I read that the candidate didn't do very well, but if you would like to have a go, the questions and answers are printed at the end of the book.

The casting in Television Productions

GOLDEN RAIN (1953)

Mrs Tuckett	DANDY NICHOLS
Syd	MYRTLE REED
Archdeacon Shearing	JOHN SALEW
Roger Strawbridge	BRIAN WORTH
Catherine Strawbridge	RONA ANDERSON
Mrs Stukeley-Mosher	PHYLLIS MONTEFIORE
Mervyn	NORMAN OSBORNE
Mr Williams	ROBERT SANSOM

A HORSEMAN RIDING BY

Paul Craddock	NIGEL HAVERS
John Rudd	GLYN HOUSTON
Hazel Potter	BERNADETTE WINDSOR
Smut Potter	MARTIN FISK
Tamer Potter	FORBES COLLINS
Meg Potter	PAM CLEMENT
Violet Potter	WENDY HOLLOWAY
Cissie Potter	VALERIE HOLLOWAY
Sam Potter	PHILIP MARTIN BROWN
Pansy Potter	KARIN FOLEY
Rose Derwent	VALERIE PHILLIPS
Will Codsall	DAVID DELVE
Edward Derwent	RICHARD BEALE
Liz Derwent	MARY CHESTER
Claire Derwent	PRUNELLA RANSOME
Agnes Matthews	JUNE MARLOW
Martha Pitts	MARYANN TURNER
Oldest inhabitant	CHARLES TURNER
Arabella Codsall	MADGE RYAN
Elinor Willoughby	SARAH PORTER
Martin Codsall	JOBY BLANSHARD
Sydney Codsall	KEVIN COPE
Arthur Pitts	ROBERT VAHEY
Gaffer Pitts	NAT PEARN
Grace Lovell	FIONA GAUNT

TO SERVE THEM ALL MY DAYS

Algy Herries	FRANK MIDDLEMASS
David Powlett-Jones	JOHN DUTTINE
Railwayman	ERIC FRANCIS
Meredith	STEPHEN JENN
Cordwainer	JOHN WELSH

Howarth	ALAN MACNAUGHTAN
Ferguson	JOHN GILL
Carter	NEIL STAGY
Ellie Herries	PATRICIA LAWRENCE
Boys: Boyer	SIMON GIPPS-KENT
Dobson	NICHOLAS LYNDHURST
Briarley	MATTHEW WATERHOUSE
and	
RICHARD HARWOOD,	SAM FREMANTLE,
ROBERT KENLEY,	NICOLAS CAMARA

DIANA

John Leigh	KEVIN McNALLY
Diana Gayelorde-Sutton	JENNY SEAGROVE
Young John	STEPHEN J. DEAN
Young Diana	PATSY KENSIT
Mark	JACK WATSON
Luke	FRED BRYANT
Reuben	IAIN ANDERS
Thirza	JUNE MARLOW
Drip	GILLIAN RAINE
Mrs. Gayelorde-Sutton	ELIZABETH BENNETT
Miss Westcott	MARY MORRIS
Yves de Royden	YVES AU BERT
Mr Priddis	PRESTON LOCKWOOD
Mr Blackler	FULTON MACKAY
Twining	JONATHAN LYNN
Mary	CHRISTINA BARRYK
Alison	LYNNE MILLER
Starkey	ADAM NORTON
Adjutant	CHRISTOPHER GOOD
Col. Ackerley	JEFFRY WICKHAM
Raoul de Royden	YVES BENEYTON
Rance	JEAN BOISSERY

AND THEN THERE WERE NONE

B.B.C. West of England Television 1956

Sir Hector Fanshaw Scott	LEWIS GEDGE
The Hon. Esmond Delahay	PAUL EDDINGTON
Iris Fanshaw Scott	ANNE MCGRATH
Topping	JUNE BARRIE
A Suffragette	JENNIFER WHITE

NO SHEPHERDS WATCHED
B.B.C. TV 1957

Cornet Player	CLINTON FFRENCH
Banjo Player	KENDRICK OWEN
P.C. Goodridge	NICHOLAS TANNER
Boxer Baker	WARREN MITCHELL
Beetie Baker	NATALIE KENT
Rocco	JAMES BELCHAMBER
Lil	PAULINE KENT
Eggyboy	BERNARD BRESSLAW
Jessie Roydon	DANDY NICHOLS
Sergeant Chadwick	RICHARD BUTLER
Monte	PETER STEPHENS

THE MAYERLING AFFAIR
B.B.C. TV 1956

Maurice Szeps (Editor/Proprietor of the *Wiener Tageblatt*)	RUPERT DAVIES
Johann Loschek (Valet to Crown Prince Rudolph)	CYRIL SHAPS
Stephanie (Crown Princess of Austria-Hungary)	BERYL BAXTER
Rudolph (Crown Prince of Austria-Hungary)	KEITH MICHELL
Bratfisch (A Viennese cab driver)	CHARLES VICTOR
Countess Larisch (Cousin of Crown Prince Rudolph)	SONIA DRESDEL
Baroness Mary Vetsera	MAI ZETTERLING
Agnes (Maid of Baroness Mary Vetsera)	DIANA BLACKWOOD
Archduke Johann Salvator	ANTHONY DAWSON
Franz Joseph 1 (Emperor of Austria-Hungary)	ANDRE VAN GYSEGHEM
Elizabeth (Empress of Austria-Hungary)	MARGARETTA SCOTT

Epilogue by Heinrich Heine, translated by Humbert Wolfe and spoken by Michael Hordern

THE DREAMING SUBURB

PEOPLE LIKE US
London Weekend Television
adapted by: James Saunders, Ian Curteis, Susan Pleat

JIM NORTON BARBARA SHELLEY JOHN DUTTINE, CAROL FRASER, PETER MACHIN, DAVID HEALY, MICHAEL LEES, JENNIFER DANIEL, MILES ANDERSON, SHIRLEY CAIN.

THE AVENUE
London Weekend Television – all cast and crew as for *PEOPLE LIKE US.*

Films–

WORMS EYE VIEW (1951)
Producer: Henry Halstead
Director: Jack Raymond
Screenplay: R.F. Delderfield, Jack Marks
Music: Tony Lowry, Tony Fones
RONALD SHINER, CARRY MARSH, JOHN BLYTHE,
BRUCE SEATON, DIGBY WOLFE, EVERLEY GREGG,
DIANA DORS, ERIC DAVIS, CHRISTINA FORREST,
WILLIAM PERCY, JONATHAN FIELD.

GLAD TIDINGS (1953)
Producer: Victor Hanbury
Director: Waiter Rilla
Screenplay: Walter Rilla
Photography: Eric Cross MUSK;
RAYMOND HUNTLEY, BARBARA KELLY, RONALD HOWARD,
JEAN LODGE, TERENCE ALEXANDER, DIANA CALDERWOOD,
LAURENCE PAYNE, ARTHUR HOWARD, BRIAN SMITH, HARRY
GREEN, ROGER MAXWELL, YVETTE WYATT, DORIS YORKE.

WHERE THERE'S A WILL (1955)
Producer: George Maynard
Director: Vernon Sewell
LESLIE DWYER THELMA RUBY DANDY NICHOLAS GEORGE
COLE KATHLEEN HARRISON MICHAEL SHEPLEY HUGH
MORTON EDWARD LEXY NORMAN MACOWAN EDWARD
WOODWARD LAM KYDD PHILIP RAY BILL :SHINE

NOW AND FOREVER (1955)
R.F. Delderfield's play *The Orchard Walls*
Producer: Mario Zampi
Director: Mario Zampi
Screenplay: R. F. Delderfield and Michael Pertwee
Photography: Erwin Hillier
Music:Stanley Black
JANETTE SCOTT, VERNON GRAY, KAY WALSH, JACK WARNER,
PAMELA BROWN, DAVID KOSSOF, WILFRED LAWSON, RONALD
SQUIRE, SONIA DRESDEL, GUY MIDDLETON, CHARLES
VICTOR, MARJORIE RHODES, MOULTRIE KELSALL, BRYAN
FORBES, MICHAEL PERTWEE, JACQUELINE CURTISS, JEAN
PATTERSON, HENRY HEWITT, HAROLD GOODWIN.

CARRY ON SERGEANT (1958)
R.F. Delderfield's play *The Bull Boys*

WILLIAM HARTNELL, BOB MONKHOUSE, SHIRLEY EATON, ERIC BARKER, DORA BRYAN, BILL OWEN, KENNETH CONNOR, CHARLES HAWTREY, KENNETH WIILIAMS, HATTIE JACQUES, TERENCE LONGDON, NORMAN ROSSINGTON, GERALD CAMPION, CYRIL CHAMBERLAIN, GORDON TANNER, FRANK FORSYTH, BASIL DIGNAM, JOHN GATRELL, ARNOLD DIAMOND, MARTIN BODDEY, IAN WHITTAKER, ANTHONY SAGAR, JOANNE STEWART, EDWARD JUDD, HELEN GROSS.

Nigel Havers and Fiona Gaunt in a scene in *A Horseman Riding By.*

Kevin McNally and Jenny Seagrove in the BBC production on *Diana.*

AFTER R.F DELDERFIELD

Readers, colleagues and family were stunned when Ron died at the age of sixty, but he and May left a legacy of an era we sometimes wish would come back. Freddy Rottey of Tielt in Belgium kept up a correspondence with May for years, and when he finally visited her at Dove Cottage, she encouraged him to choose any of Ron's books from his shelf which started his collection of Delderfield memorabilia.

Below is also a letter May Delderfield wrote to her carer, and at the bottom it very touchingly says 'Mrs. Delderfield, wife of R.F. Delderfield.' I think, Mrs. Delderfield deserves as much recognition as her famous husband because without her and her unstinting support, he might not have become the well-loved story teller we know. She died on the 4th of May 1988.

When you come on a pilgrimage to Sidmouth do have a look at the splendid new memorial stone and plaque organised by the Sid Vale Association to whose unveiling the Reverend Handel Bennett had kindly invited me. At first, the Association had planned to move the old memorial stone from further up the hill, which was threatening to fall into the sea. It turned out to be far too heavy, and thus was the affection for Sidmouth's famous resident that they had soon collected enough money for a new rock of Dartmoor granite which was moved to a safer position halfway up the hill on the way to Peak Cottage and the Gazebo where Ron had lived.

So still no scandals or juicy titbits, I am afraid, but that is not what the friends of R.F. Delderfield are looking for. As one of the big publishers had put it in his rejection letter: 'Not enough sex and violence.'

But that is just how we like it; that is why R.F. Delderfield is still remembered with love, joy and a big, broad smile; remembered for his beautiful stories so eloquently told, the vivid and wonderful descriptions of East Devon and his characters so human with their foibles, tears and laughter. They lived at a time and in a world we hanker after, when people were still close to each other and realised that in the great scheme of things we all depend on one another.

If this centenary edition entices people to re-visit or rediscover the R.F. Delderfield sagas, maybe we can recover some of the magic.
Now that would be a worthy tribute!

Memorial stone and plaques in Sidmouth.

A Memorial Service will be
held for Mr. R. F. Delderfield
at St. Bride's Church, Fleet Street,
London, E.C.4 on Wednesday,
July 19th at 12.30 p.m.

Dec. 14, 1957.

"DOVE COTTAGE"
MANOR RD,
SIDMOUTH. EX1031

Dear Diana,

I've known a large number of
people in my life but you are one
of the most wonderful Christians I've
ever met and I thank God for
lending you to me.

Please accept this gift with my
love and thanks.
I hope you have a wonderful
Christmas and New Year.

love from
May Delderfield

Mrs Delerfield
— wife of R. F. Delerfield

Letter from May Delderfield to Di Tapley

231

MASTERMIND 1983/84

Subject – The Epic Novels of R.F. Delderfield

Questions:

1. In *God Is An Englishman*, what did Adam Swann find in the broken casket during the clash at the Ranee's palace?
2. What was the name of the college where Adam Swann trained as a cadet?
3. In *God Is An Englishman*, what was the name of the dog that Henrietta Rawlinson took with her when she escaped from her father's house?
4. In *Theirs Was The Kingdom*, Alexander Swann was promoted by Kitchener following an incident on a Nile steamer. Who was the Scottish corporal who died in the incident?
5. In *God Is An Englishman*, Edith Wadsworth met her future husband when he worked under her as a waggoner. What was his true occupation at this time?
6. In *Theirs Was The Kingdom*, Stella Swann's first marriage was annulled. Who was her second husband?
7. In *Theirs Was The Kingdom*, the morning after his eighteenth birthday, George Swann witnessed a savage fight between two women. Name one of them.
8. In *God Is An Englishman*, in what circumstances did Adam Swann receive the injuries that led to him losing his leg?
9. In *Give Us This Day*, which member of the Swann family was known by the older waggoners as the 'New Broom'?
10. suggested by Eric McKenzie but not used by the BBC
11. In *Give Us This Day*, after his marriage, George Swann became involved with the wife of a Scottish industrialist. What was her name?
12. In *The Green Gauntlet*, what weapon did Henry Pitts use to help capture the escaped German prisoner-of-war at Shallowford House?
13. In *The Green Gauntlet*, for what purpose did Jumbo Bellchamber want to buy Low Coombe, the tattiest farm on the Shallowford Estate?

14. In *The Green Gauntlet*, how did Claire ensure the safety of her grandchild Vanessa at the cost of her own life in the flood?

15. In *A Horseman Riding By*, what other event did Paul Craddock note in his estate diary the day his wife gave birth to twins?

16. In *A Horseman Riding By*, what was the nature of the injury that Paul Craddock had sustained in the Boer War?

17. According to *A Horseman Riding By*, what was the trade of Joshua, Paul Craddock's father before he became a scrap merchant?

18. In *A Horseman Riding By*, Claire Craddock's fourth child was officially named Karen. What was the child's more familiar nickname?

19. In *A Horseman Riding By*, Ikey Palfrey, was fatally wounded in the First World War. How did this happen?

20. In *A Horseman Riding By*, which one of the farms on the Shallowford Estate was supposed to be cursed?

21. In *To Serve Them All My Days*, what was the name of the boy who faked an epileptic fit on David Powlett-Jones's second day at Bamfylde?

22. In *To Serve Them All My Days*, what derogatory nickname did Carter give Havelock House that caused a serious quarrel between Carter and Powlett-Jones?

23. submitted but not chosen by the BBC

24. In *To Serve Them All My Days*, where did Christine and Powlett-Jones spend a holiday together before they were married?

25. In *The Dreaming Suburb*, why was Jim Carver unable to be with his wife when she died of Spanish 'flu?

26. submitted but not chosen by the BBC

27. In *The Dreaming Suburb*, by what name was Tom Tappertitt's wife known in the circus?

28. *The Dreaming Suburb* is set in an avenue in a London suburb. What is the full name of the Avenue?

29. In *The Avenue Goes To War*, for what action was Ted Hartnell awarded the George Medal?

30. In *The Avenue Goes To War*, when Archie Carver was released from prison, whom did he find waiting for him?

Answers to Mastermind questions:

1)   *Jewellery/ a ruby necklace*
2)   *Addiscombe College*
3)   *Twitch*
4)   *McTavish*
5)   *Professional thief*
6)   *Denzel Fawcett*
7)   *Laura Broadbent or Lizzie Broadbent*
8)   *In a railway accident*
9)   *George Swann*
10)   —
11)   *Lady Barbara Lockerbie*
12)   *A pitchfork*
13)   *He proposed to make it into a camping and caravan site*
14)   *She tied the girl to a tree with webbing from a sofa*
15)   *The death of the Reverend Horace Bull*
16)   *Smashed knee-cap*
17)   *Plumber*
18)   *Whiz or Whizzo*
19)   *He picked up a booby-trapped pickelhaube (German dress helmet)*
20)   *'Four Winds'*
21)   *(Chadwick S.) Boyer*
22)   *The Kremlin*
23)   —
24)   *At Windermere in the Lake District*
25)   *He was serving with the British Army of occupation in Germany*
26)   —
27)   *Audrey the Amazon*
28)   *Manor Park Avenue*
29)   *For maintaining the morale of shipwrecked sailors adrift in a boat by playing his harmonica*
30)   *Elaine Fraser*